On a Mission to Love

Rosary Meditations for Children and Families

Ruah Woods
PRESS

In accord with the *Code of Canon Law*, I hereby grant the *Imprimatur* ("Permission to Publish") regarding the manuscript entitled:

> *On a Mission to Love: Rosary Meditations for Children and Families*
>
> Most Reverend Joseph R. Binzer
> Auxiliary Bishop
> Vicar General
> Archdiocese of Cincinnati
> Cincinnati, Ohio
> June 19th, 2018

The *Imprimatur* ("Permission to Publish") is a declaration that a book or pamphlet is considered to be free of doctrinal or moral error. It is not implied that those who have granted the *Imprimatur* agree with the contents, opinions or statements expressed.

Copyright © 2018 by Debbie Staresinic
All rights reserved.

ISBN: 978-1-947008-10-6

Excerpt from Pope John Paul II, XVIII World Youth Day, 13 March 2003, used with permission of the © LIBRERIA EDITRICE VATICANA.

Photo of Pope St. John Paul II © L'Osservatore Romano. Used with permission.

Excerpts from How to Pray the Rosary © 2018, United States Conference of Catholic Bishops, Washington, DC. Used with permission. All rights reserved. No portion of this text may be reproduced by any means without permission in writing from the copyright owner.

Scripture texts in this work are taken from the New American Bible, revised edition © 2010, 1991, 1986, 1970, Confraternity of Christian Doctrine, Washington, D.C., and are used by permission of the copyright owner. All rights reserved. No part of the New American Bible may be reproduced in any form without permission in writing from the copyright owner.

Interior images by BRADI BARTH © www.bradi-barth.org.
Used with permission.

Project Manager: Mike Fontecchio

Cover Illustration, Design and Typesetting: Meghan Klare-Florkowski

How to Pray the Rosary Image Design: Elizabeth C. Klare

Editors: Dr. Joan Kingsland and Stephen Kovacs

Printed in the United States of America.
Published in the United States by Ruah Woods Press.

> All proceeds support Ruah Woods Press
> THEOLOGY OF THE BODY K-12 CURRICULUM

Dedication

To Mary, our Mother in Heaven,
who helps us to love as Jesus loves

*Our Lady of Fatima
asks us
to pray the Rosary
each day.*

This book belongs to

_____

I am a gift.
I am a child of God.
I am unique and unrepeatable.
I am loved beyond measure.
God invites me to share His
love with everyone around me.
I am part of His mission.
I am made to LOVE!

*"Let the children come to me;
do not prevent them, for the kingdom of God
belongs to such as these."*

Mark 10:14

INSIDE THIS BOOK

Words from Pope St. John Paul II.................................. 8

A Letter to the Children.................................. 9

Welcome to Parents and Teachers........................, 10

A Decade a Day Weekly Schedule........................ 11

About the Rosary.................................. 12

Leading the Rosary: A Decade a Day.................. 13

Rosary Prayers.................................. 14

Rosary Visual 15

The Joyful Mysteries.................................. 17

The Sorrowful Mysteries.................................. 29

The Glorious Mysteries.................................. 41

The Luminous Mysteries.................................. 53

About the Author.................................. 64

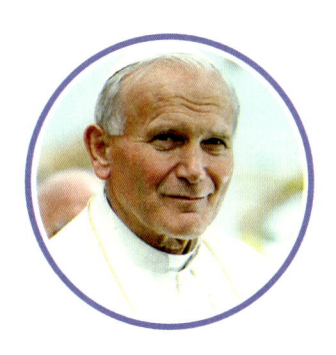

"Today, my dear young people, I am also, in spirit, handing you the Rosary beads. Through prayer and meditation on the mysteries, Mary leads you safely towards her Son!"

–Pope St. John Paul II

Feast of Our Lady of Fatima
May 13, 2018

Dear Children,

On the day you were baptized, you began your new life in Jesus and became a member of His Church. On that special day, you were assigned a mighty mission. Your mission in life is to love. God gave us the Rosary as a special gift to help us on our journey. The Rosary helps us to think about the life of Jesus with the tender guidance of His Mother Mary. She helps us to love as Jesus loves and to share the Good News of His love with the world. May God bless you on your mission!

Your friend in the Rosary,

Mrs. Staresinic

Mrs. Staresinic

YOUR MISSION IN LIFE IS TO LOVE

WELCOME TO PARENTS AND TEACHERS

Thank you for your role in bringing the Rosary and Pope St. John Paul II's teaching to your children. These pages offer suggestions for how this book may be used to bring families, classes, or individual children to a deeper devotion to the Rosary, while at the same time meditating on the concepts taught by Pope St. John Paul II that are known as "Theology of the Body."

FRUITS OF PRAYING WITH THIS BOOK

The reflections in this book cultivate awareness and gratitude for the dignity of every person as a unique and unrepeatable gift from God to be embraced and upheld in all that we do. With Jesus and Mary as our models, the prayers and reflections are intended to affirm and awaken our vocation to love and our call to make a gift of ourselves.

HOW TO PRAY THE ROSARY

If you are new to praying the Rosary, you may wish to first refer to pages 14 and 15 for a diagram of the Rosary and its accompanying prayers.

PRAYING THE ROSARY: A DECADE A DAY

This book contains all four sets of Rosary Mysteries: Joyful, Sorrowful, Glorious, and Luminous. Each set contains five individual mysteries, making twenty Mysteries in total.

To make the daily Rosary an achievable goal for young families and classrooms, this book is designed to facilitate praying one mystery of the Rosary per day. If taking this approach, you might choose to employ the suggested weekly schedule on the next page. This book may just as easily be used to pray a full set of mysteries per day, or even a full Rosary per day (all four sets).

A DECADE A DAY WEEKLY SCHEDULE

Week One
JOYFUL MYSTERIES

Monday:	The Annunciation	(pages 18-19)
Tuesday:	The Visitation	(pages 20-21)
Wednesday:	The Nativity	(pages 22-23)
Thursday:	The Presentation of the Lord	(pages 24-25)
Friday:	The Finding of Jesus in the Temple	(pages 26-27)

Week Two
SORROWFUL MYSTERIES

Monday:	The Agony in the Garden	(pages 30-31)
Tuesday:	The Scourging at the Pillar	(pages 32-33)
Wednesday:	The Crowning with Thorns	(pages 34-35)
Thursday:	The Carrying of the Cross	(pages 36-37)
Friday:	The Crucifixion	(pages 38-39)

Week Three
GLORIOUS MYSTERIES

Monday:	The Resurrection	(pages 42-43)
Tuesday:	The Ascension	(pages 44-45)
Wednesday:	The Descent of the Holy Spirit	(pages 46-47)
Thursday:	The Assumption	(pages 48-49)
Friday:	The Coronation of Mary	(pages 50-51)

Week Four
LUMINOUS MYSTERIES

Monday:	The Baptism of the Lord	(pages 54-55)
Tuesday:	The Wedding Feast at Cana	(pages 56-57)
Wednesday:	The Proclamation of the Kingdom	(pages 58-59)
Thursday:	The Transfiguration	(pages 60-61)
Friday:	The Institution of the Eucharist	(pages 62-63)

ABOUT THE ROSARY

"The Rosary is a Scripture-based prayer. It begins with the Apostles' Creed, which summarizes the great mysteries of the Catholic faith. The Our Father, which introduces each mystery, is from the Gospels. The first part of the Hail Mary is the angel's words announcing Christ's birth and Elizabeth's greeting to Mary. St. Pius V officially added the second part of the Hail Mary. The Mysteries of the Rosary center on the events of Christ's life.

There are four sets of Mysteries: Joyful, Sorrowful, Glorious and - added by Pope John Paul II in 2002 - the Luminous.

The repetition in the Rosary is meant to lead one into restful and contemplative prayer related to each Mystery. The gentle repetition of the words helps us to enter into the silence of our hearts, where Christ's spirit dwells. The Rosary can be said privately or with a group."

Excerpt from How to Pray the Rosary, USCCB

LEADING THE ROSARY: A DECADE A DAY

This method will usually require less than five minutes.

A PARENT, A TEACHER, OR AN OLDER CHILD BEGINS BY:

- Leading the group in making the Sign of the Cross.
- The leader then announces aloud the mystery to be prayed and its corresponding virtue.
- The group responds by praying the Our Father together.
- Next, the same or another leader reads the first reflection statement.
- The group responds by praying the Hail Mary together.
- This process is repeated ten times until each reflection statement has been read.
- After the tenth Hail Mary, the group prays the Glory Be together.
- Then the group prays The Fatima Prayer.
- Optional: All pray the Hail Holy Queen (Salve Regina)
- The group concludes by making the Sign of the Cross together.

For supplemental information on praying the Rosary please visit www.missiontolove.org

ROSARY PRAYERS

Apostles' Creed

I believe in God, the Father Almighty, Creator of Heaven and earth; and in Jesus Christ, His only Son, Our Lord, Who was conceived by the Holy Spirit, born of the Virgin Mary, suffered under Pontius Pilate, was crucified, died, and was buried. He descended into hell; the third day He arose again from the dead; He ascended into Heaven, and is seated at the right hand of God, the Father Almighty; from thence He shall come to judge the living and the dead. I believe in the Holy Spirit, the holy Catholic Church, the communion of saints, the forgiveness of sins, the resurrection of the body, and life everlasting. Amen.

Our Father

Our Father, Who art in Heaven, hallowed be Thy name. Thy kingdom come. Thy will be done, on earth as it is in Heaven. Give us this day our daily bread. And forgive us our trespasses, as we forgive those who trespass against us. And lead us not into temptation, but deliver us from evil. Amen.

Hail Mary

Hail Mary, full of grace, the Lord is with thee. Blessed art thou among women, and blessed is the fruit of thy womb, Jesus. Holy Mary, Mother of God, pray for us sinners, now, and at the hour of our death. Amen.

Glory Be

Glory be to the Father, and to the Son, and to the Holy Spirit. As it was in the beginning, is now, and ever shall be, world without end. Amen.

Fatima Prayer

O my Jesus, forgive us our sins, save us from the fires of hell, and lead all souls to Heaven, especially those in most need of Thy mercy.

Hail Holy Queen

Hail, holy Queen, mother of mercy, our life, our sweetness, and our hope. To you we cry, poor banished children of Eve; to you we send up our sighs, mourning and weeping in this valley of tears. Turn, then, most gracious advocate, your eyes of mercy toward us; and after this, our exile, show unto us the blessed fruit of your womb, Jesus. O clement, O loving, O sweet Virgin Mary.

How to Pray the Rosary

- 10 Hail Marys
- Glory Be, then Fatima Prayer
- Announce 4th Mystery, then pray Our Father
- 10 Hail Marys
- Glory Be, then Fatima Prayer
- Announce 5th Mystery, then pray Our Father
- 10 Hail Marys
- Announce 3rd Mystery, then pray Our Father
- Glory Be, then Fatima Prayer
- 10 Hail Marys
- Announce 2nd Mystery, then pray Our Father
- Glory Be, then Fatima Prayer
- 10 Hail Marys
- Glory Be, Fatima Prayer, and Hail Holy Queen
- continue this direction
- Finish
- Announce 1st Mystery, then pray Our Father
- Glory Be
- 3 Hail Marys
- Our Father
- Start — Make the Sign of the Cross and say the Apostles' Creed.

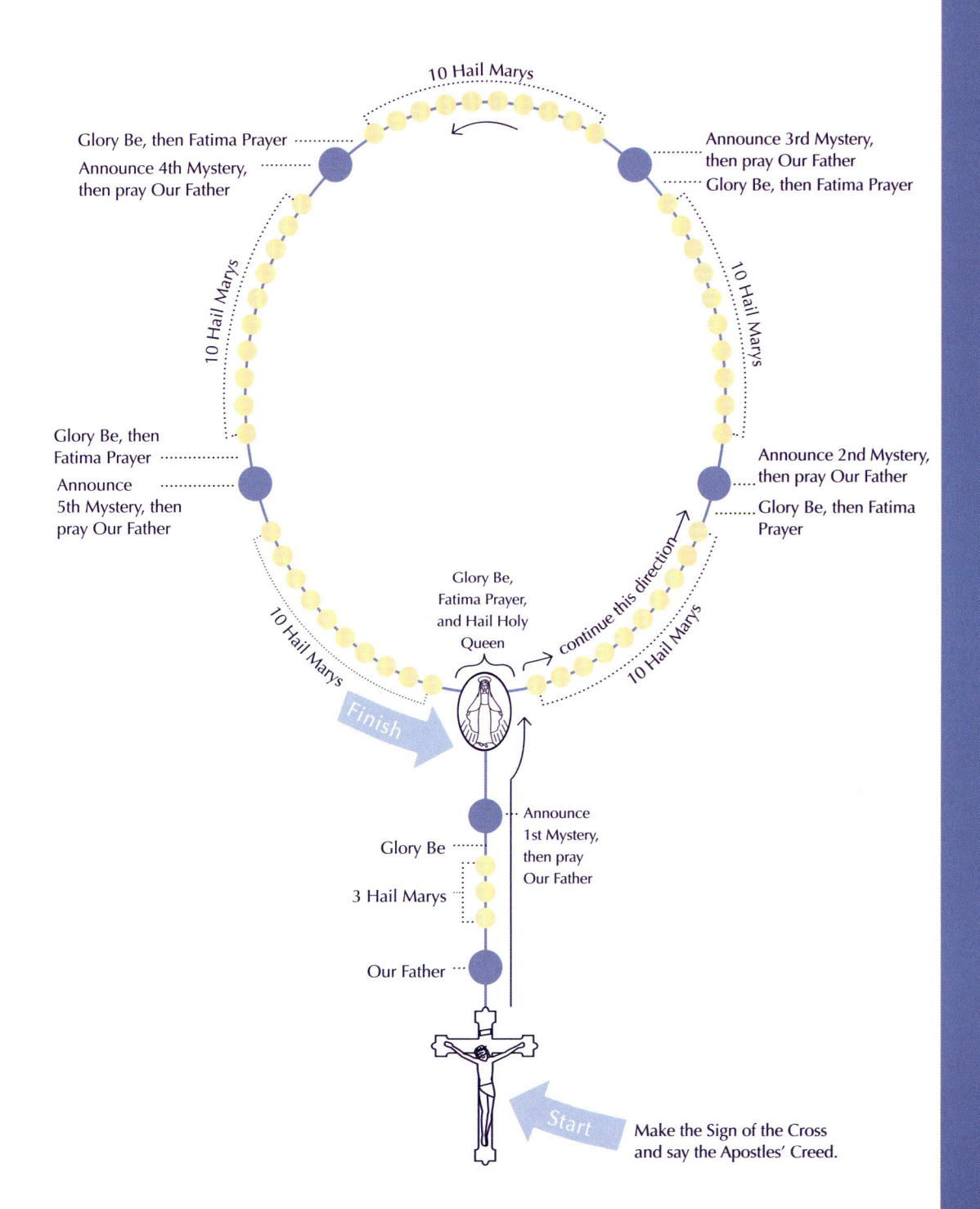

15

The Joyful Mysteries

Monday & Saturday

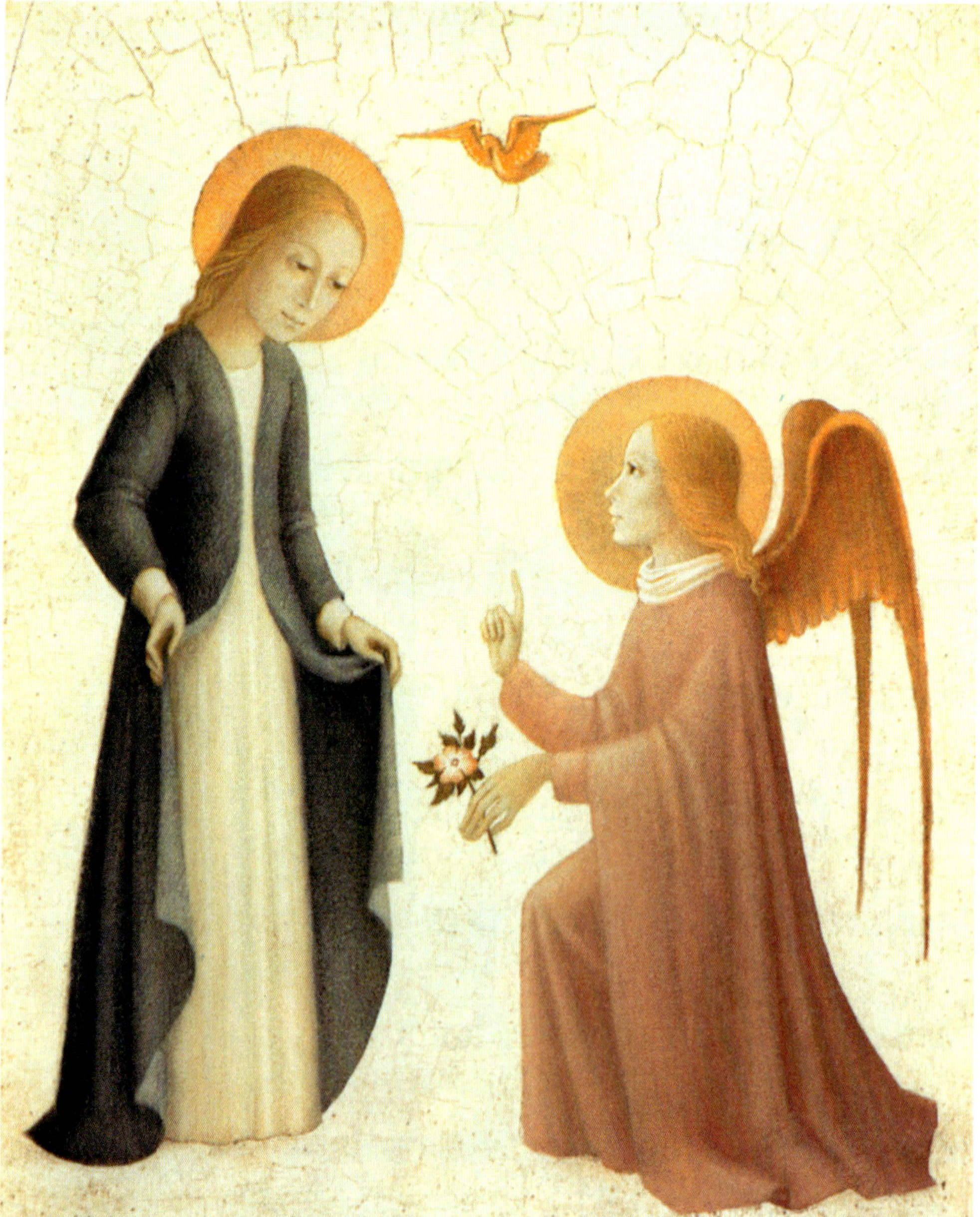

The Annunciation

Virtue: Love of God

OUR FATHER

Long ago, in the tiny town of Nazareth, God sent an angel to a girl named Mary. *HAIL MARY...*

The angel Gabriel told Mary that God wanted her to be the mother of His Son. *HAIL MARY...*

Mary knew that God is a loving Father, so she trusted in His love for her. *HAIL MARY...*

Mary said yes to God's will. *HAIL MARY...*

God is our Father too, and He loves us very much. *HAIL MARY...*

God made us in His image, which gives us great dignity. *HAIL MARY...*

God gave us a body, which we can see, and a soul, which we cannot see. *HAIL MARY...*

Our body and soul work together so we can think, choose, and love. *HAIL MARY...*

God, our loving Father, thank you for the gift of life and for creating us in your image. *HAIL MARY...*

God, our loving Father, please help us to always be respectful of ourselves and one another. *HAIL MARY...*

GLORY BE...FATIMA PRAYER (OH MY JESUS)...

The Joyful Mysteries

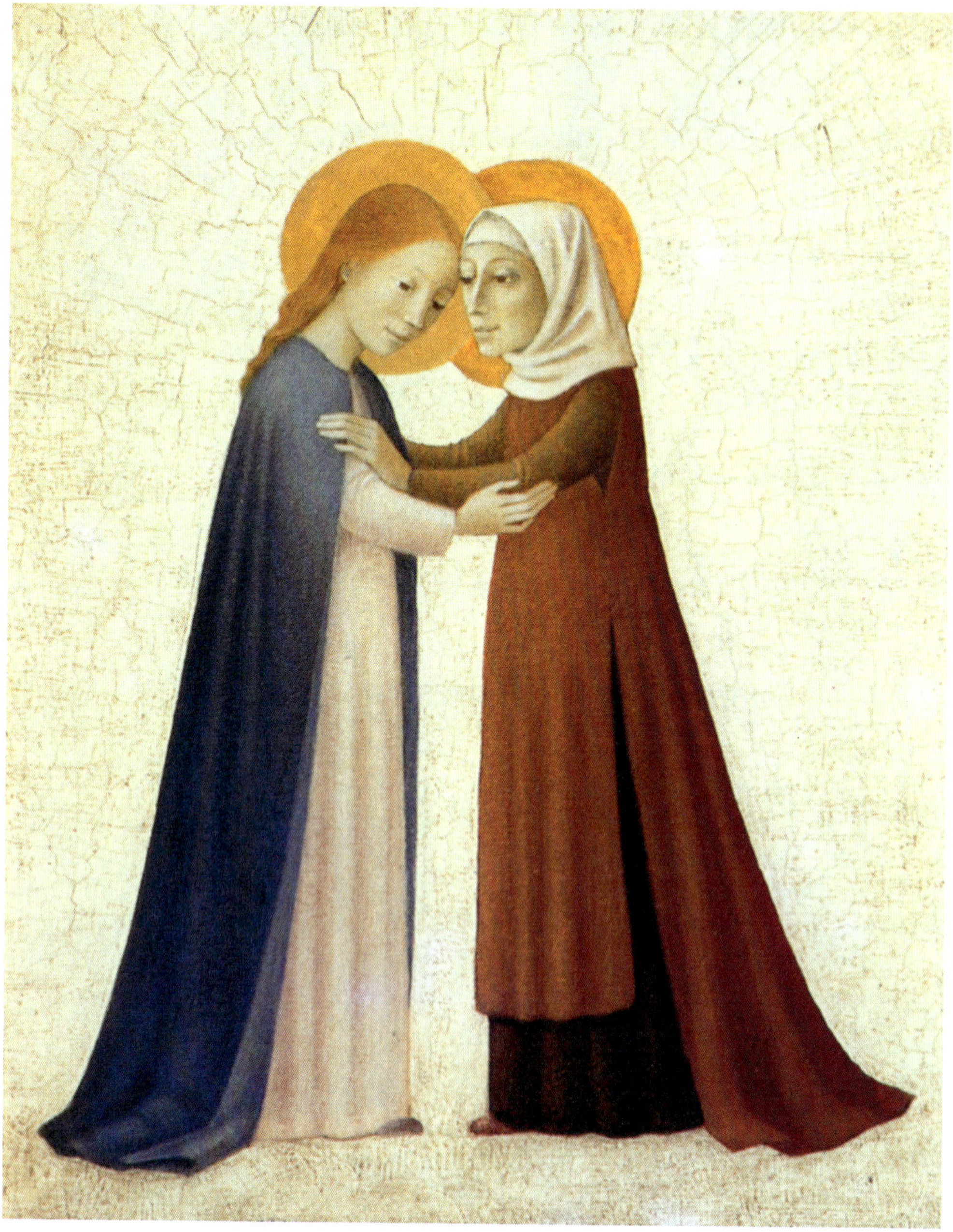

The Visitation

Virtue: Love of Neighbor

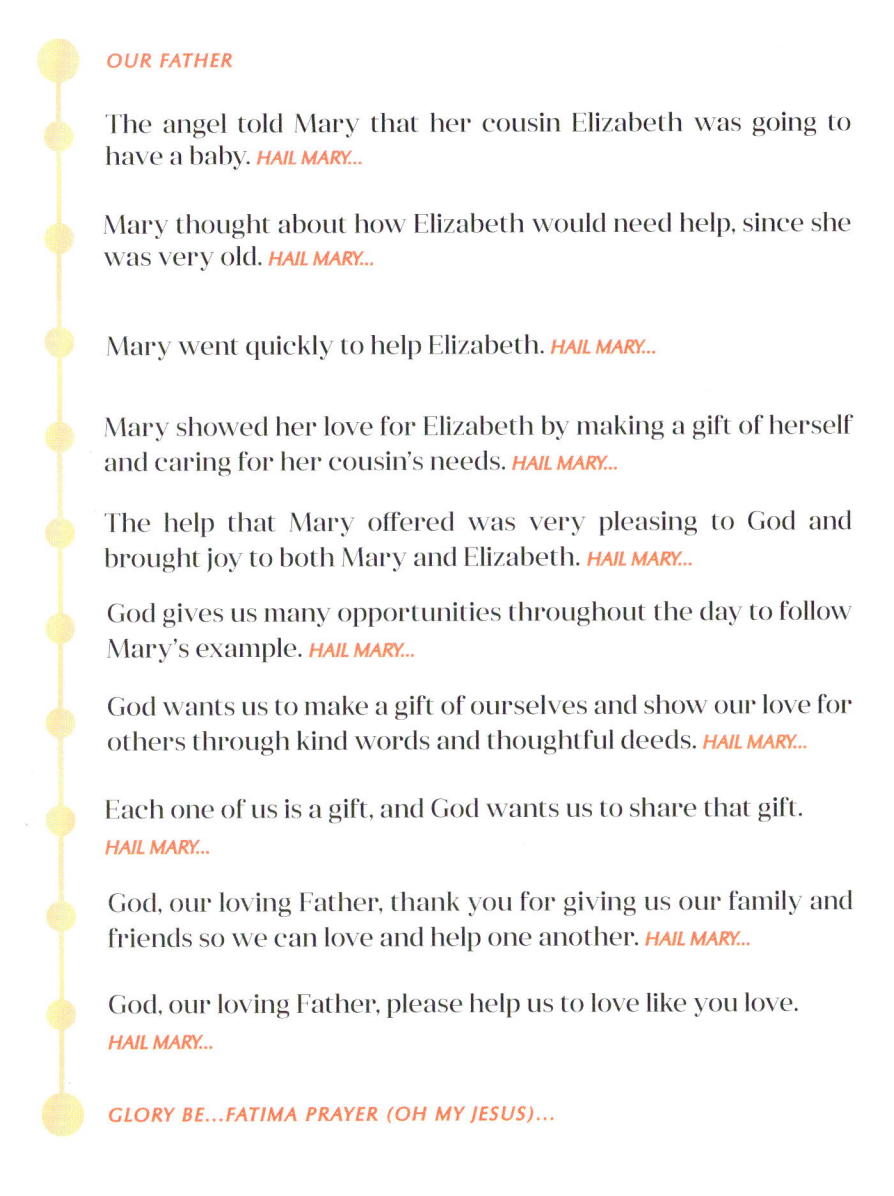

OUR FATHER

The angel told Mary that her cousin Elizabeth was going to have a baby. *HAIL MARY...*

Mary thought about how Elizabeth would need help, since she was very old. *HAIL MARY...*

Mary went quickly to help Elizabeth. *HAIL MARY...*

Mary showed her love for Elizabeth by making a gift of herself and caring for her cousin's needs. *HAIL MARY...*

The help that Mary offered was very pleasing to God and brought joy to both Mary and Elizabeth. *HAIL MARY...*

God gives us many opportunities throughout the day to follow Mary's example. *HAIL MARY...*

God wants us to make a gift of ourselves and show our love for others through kind words and thoughtful deeds. *HAIL MARY...*

Each one of us is a gift, and God wants us to share that gift. *HAIL MARY...*

God, our loving Father, thank you for giving us our family and friends so we can love and help one another. *HAIL MARY...*

God, our loving Father, please help us to love like you love. *HAIL MARY...*

GLORY BE...FATIMA PRAYER (OH MY JESUS)...

The Joyful Mysteries

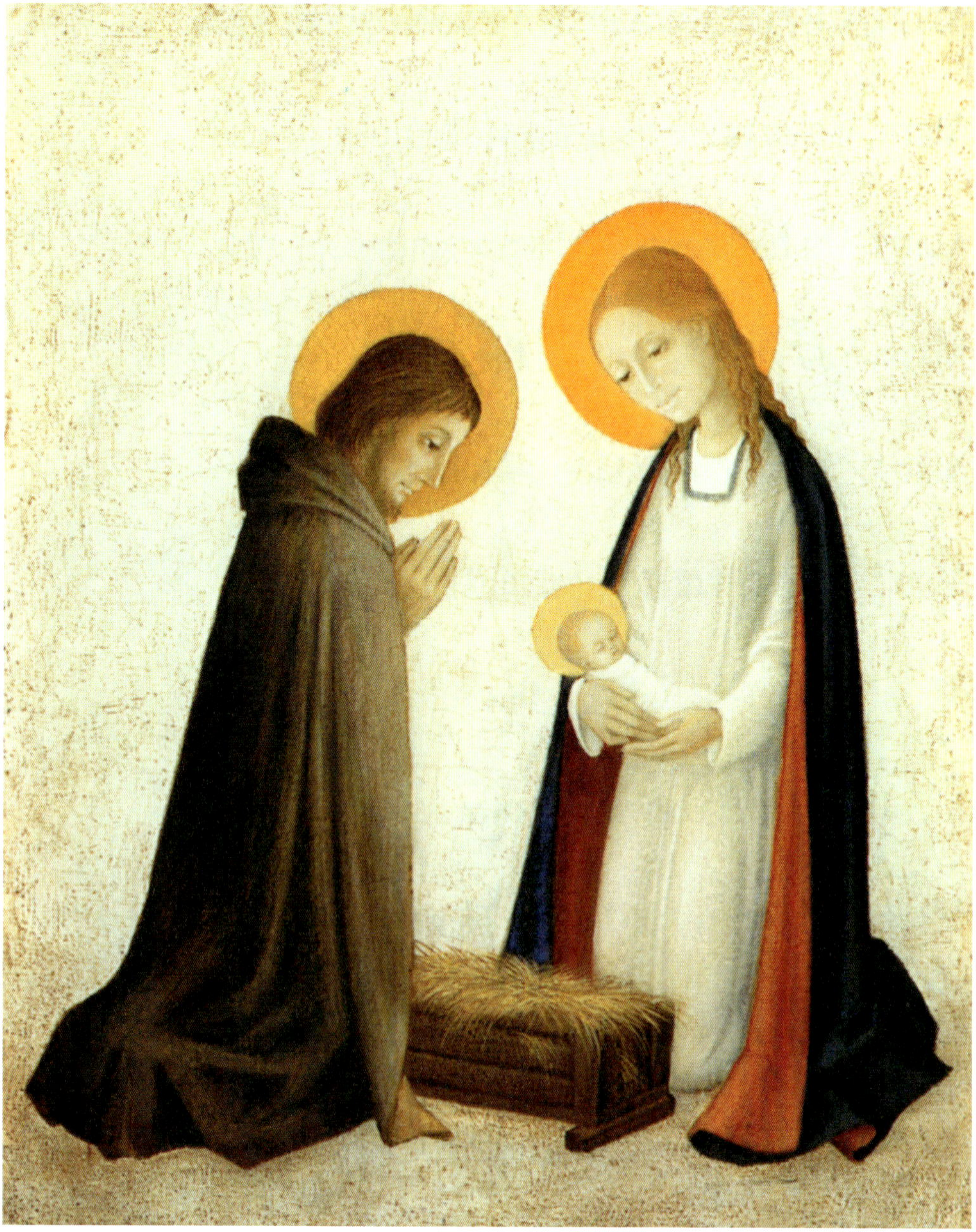

The Nativity

Virtue: Humility

OUR FATHER

God wanted us to know how much He loves us, so He sent Jesus to us. *HAIL MARY...*

God made Himself visible by coming into this world as a baby. *HAIL MARY...*

Mary gave birth to the baby Jesus not in a castle but in a lowly manger. *HAIL MARY...*

God made Himself small to make it easier for us to understand Him, welcome Him, and love Him. *HAIL MARY...*

God took on human nature to show us the dignity of all people and our place above the rest of creation. *HAIL MARY...*

Mary, Joseph, and the shepherds experienced God's love by seeing, hearing, touching, and kissing Jesus. *HAIL MARY...*

God gave us our senses so that we could experience His love in many ways. *HAIL MARY...*

We worship and praise God with our senses at Mass; we smell incense, hear prayers, taste the Eucharist, touch the holy water, and see the priest and all the people. *HAIL MARY...*

God, our loving Father, thank you for sending us the little baby Jesus so that we could know your love for us. *HAIL MARY...*

God, our loving Father, please deepen our desire to spend time with you so we can come to know you and all you have planned for us. *HAIL MARY...*

GLORY BE...FATIMA PRAYER (OH MY JESUS)...

The Joyful Mysteries

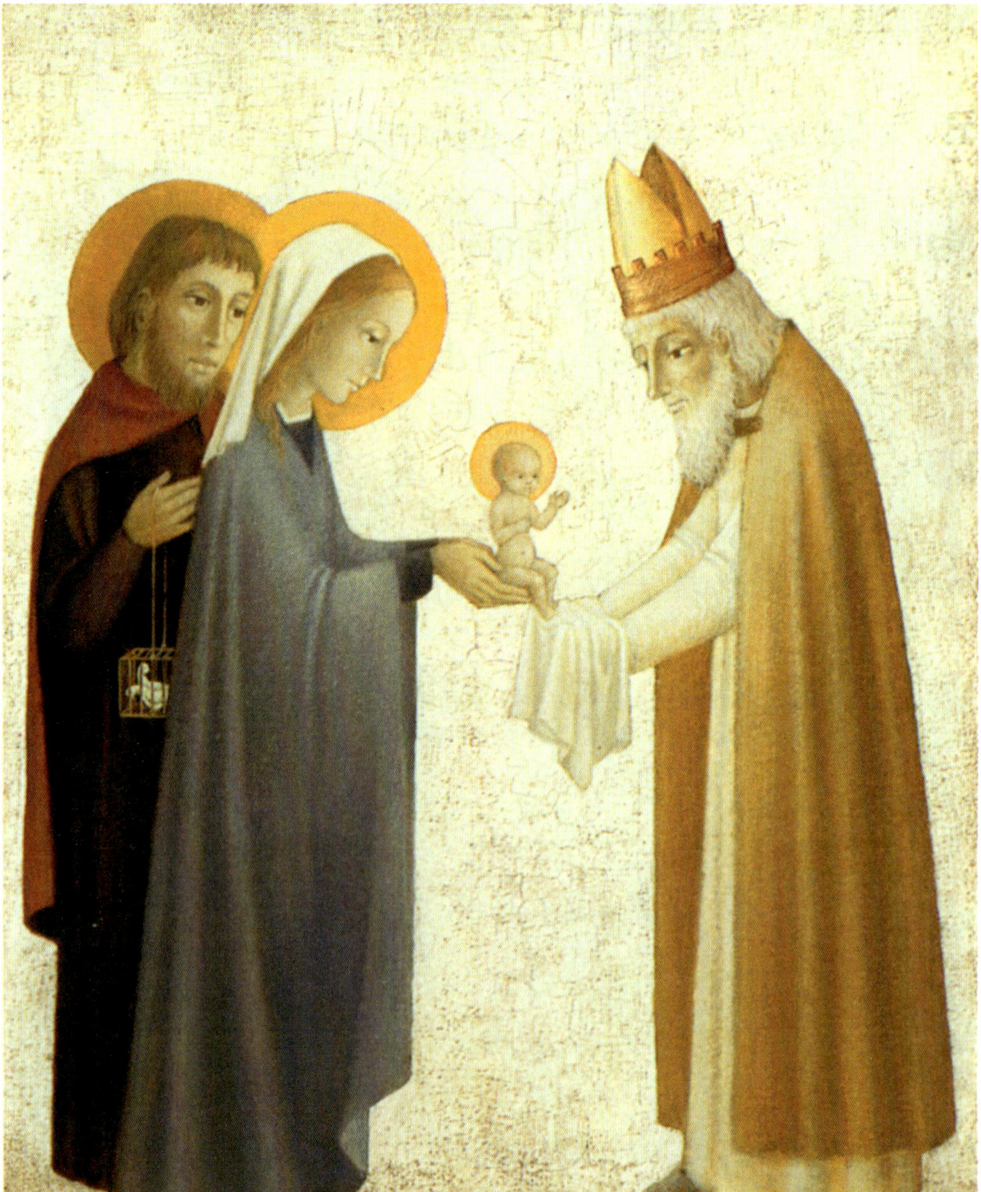

The Presentation

Virtue: Sharing Jesus With Others

OUR FATHER

Forty days after Jesus was born, Mary and Joseph took Jesus to the Temple to offer Him to God. *HAIL MARY...*

In the Temple, they met a man named Simeon and a woman named Anna. *HAIL MARY...*

Simeon knew that Jesus was sent by the Father as our Savior; he took Jesus into his arms and thanked God. *HAIL MARY...*

Anna told people about Jesus and thanked God for sending us a savior. *HAIL MARY...*

Just as Mary and Joseph brought the gift of Jesus to others, we are meant to bring Jesus to others. *HAIL MARY...*

Before we can bring Jesus to others, we have to open our hearts to receive Him ourselves. *HAIL MARY...*

God doesn't want us to be alone, so He gives us family, friends, and the Church. *HAIL MARY...*

We call the Church "Our Mother," and we are brothers and sisters in her. *HAIL MARY...*

God, our loving Father, thank you for giving us family, friends, and the Church. *HAIL MARY...*

God, our loving Father, please help us to love Jesus and to bring Him to others. *HAIL MARY...*

GLORY BE...FATIMA PRAYER (OH MY JESUS)...

The Joyful Mysteries

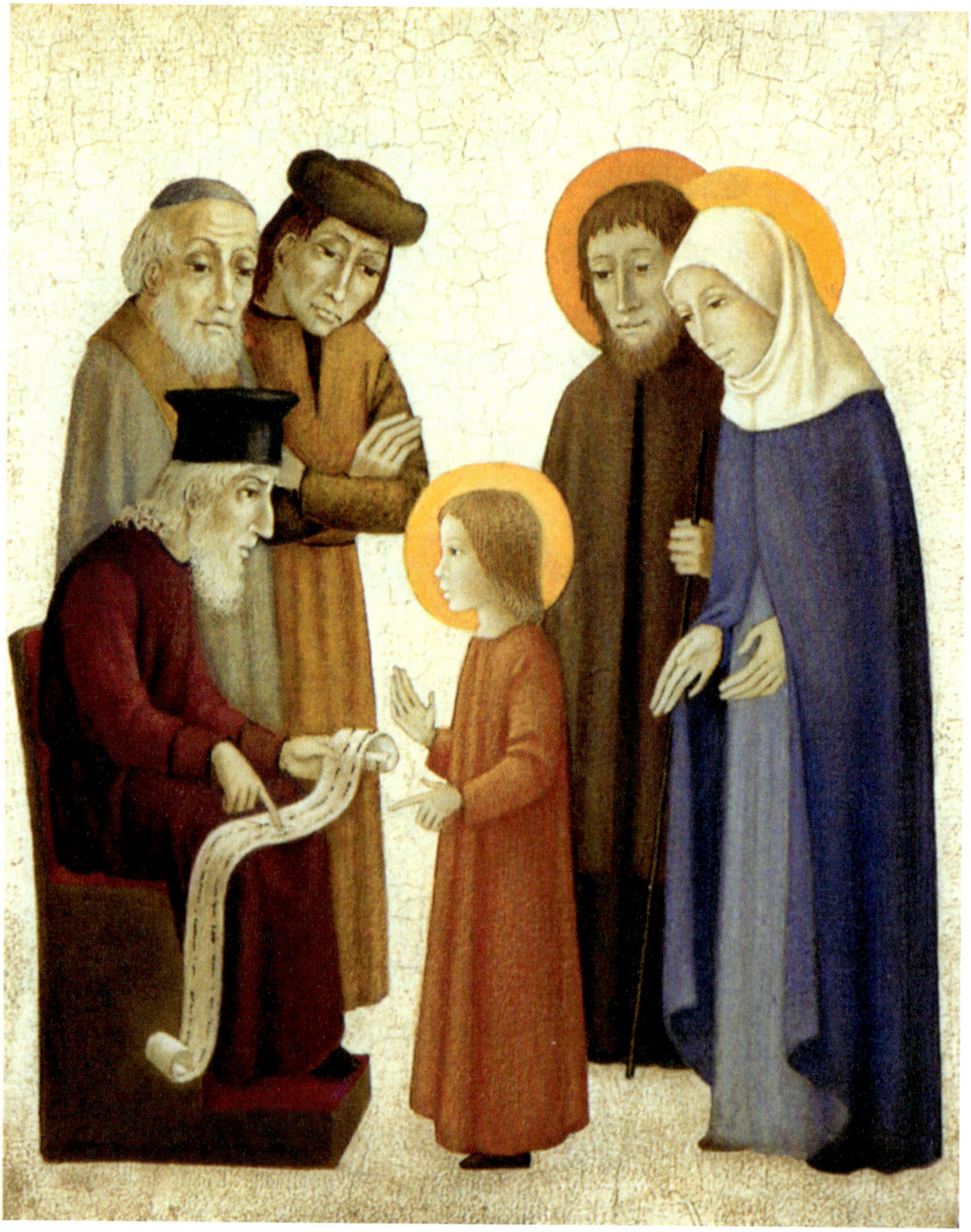

The Finding in the Temple

Virtue: Hope

The Joyful Mysteries

OUR FATHER

When Jesus was twelve, He traveled with Mary and Joseph to Jerusalem. *HAIL MARY...*

On the way home, Jesus stayed behind, but Mary and Joseph didn't know it. *HAIL MARY...*

After searching for Jesus for three days, Mary and Joseph found Him in the Temple praying and asking questions of the teachers. *HAIL MARY...*

Jesus was doing the work that His Father in Heaven sent Him to do. *HAIL MARY...*

God entrusted Jesus with a mighty mission. *HAIL MARY...*

Jesus' mission was to help us get to Heaven by teaching us how to love God and our neighbor. *HAIL MARY...*

Jesus is with us every day to help us act like He did. *HAIL MARY...*

Jesus wants all of us to be happy with Him now and forever in Heaven. *HAIL MARY...*

God, our loving Father, thank you for the mission you gave to Jesus. *HAIL MARY...*

God, our loving Father, please help us to do what Jesus teaches us to do through His words and example. *HAIL MARY...*

GLORY BE...FATIMA PRAYER (OH MY JESUS)...

The Sorrowful Mysteries

Tuesday & Friday

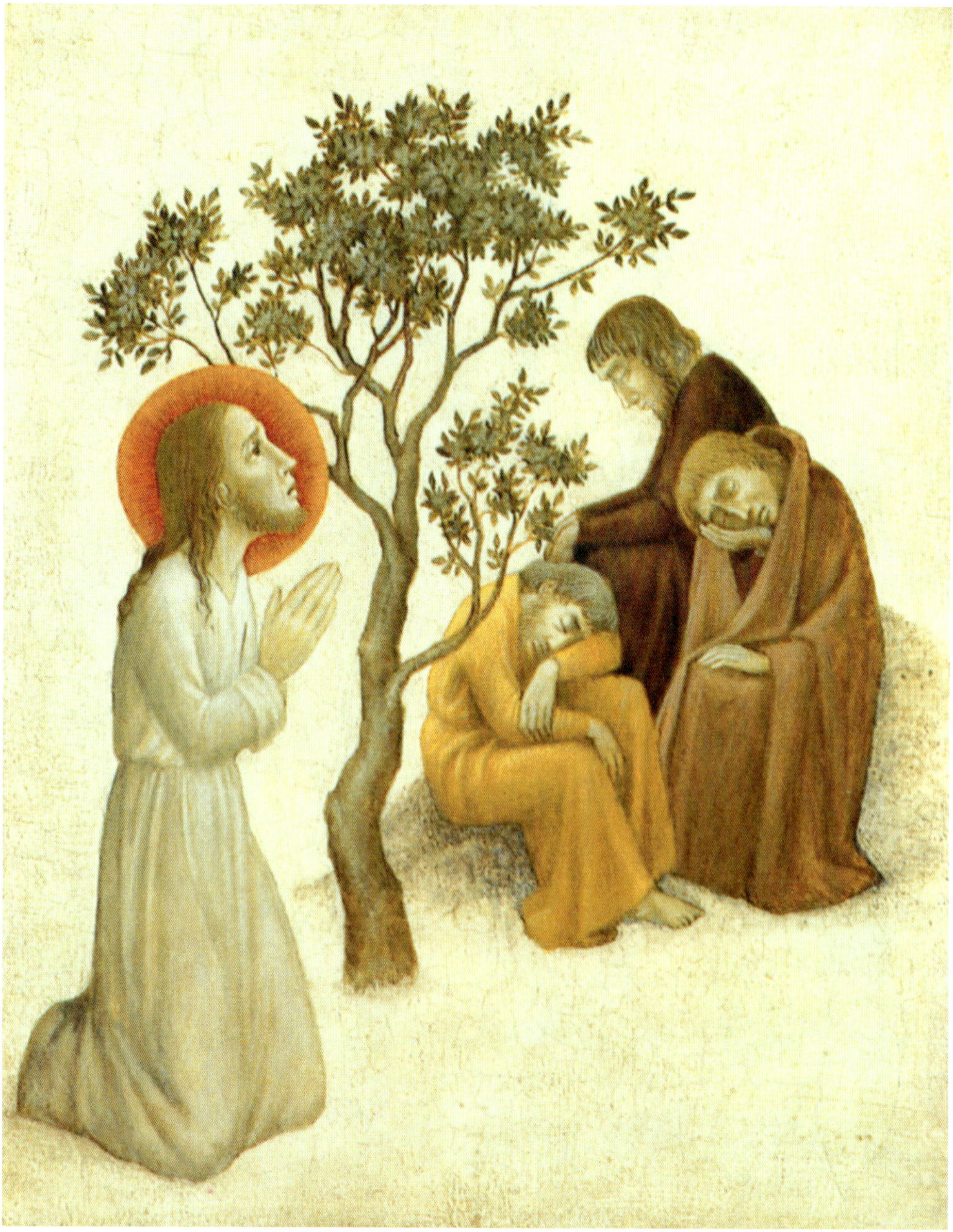

The Agony in the Garden

Virtue: Obedience

OUR FATHER

After sharing His last meal with His apostles, Jesus went to the garden to pray. *HAIL MARY...*

Jesus asked Peter, James, and John to stay awake and pray with Him, but they fell asleep. *HAIL MARY...*

Jesus knew that He would suffer and die the next day. *HAIL MARY...*

It was hard for Jesus to suffer so much and to die, but He lovingly promised to accept His Father's plan for Him. *HAIL MARY...*

When Jesus finished praying, the soldiers came and took Him away. *HAIL MARY...*

Out of love and obedience, Jesus made a gift of Himself to His Father and to each one of us. *HAIL MARY...*

Jesus accepted His suffering so that we could be freed from our sins. *HAIL MARY...*

Sin hurts our relationship with God and makes us unhappy; obedience to God brings us true happiness. *HAIL MARY...*

Lord Jesus, thank you for suffering and dying for us so that our sins could be forgiven. *HAIL MARY...*

God, our loving Father, please help us to always remember that sin will hurt our relationship with Jesus and make us unhappy. *HAIL MARY...*

GLORY BE...FATIMA PRAYER (OH MY JESUS)...

The Sorrowful Mysteries

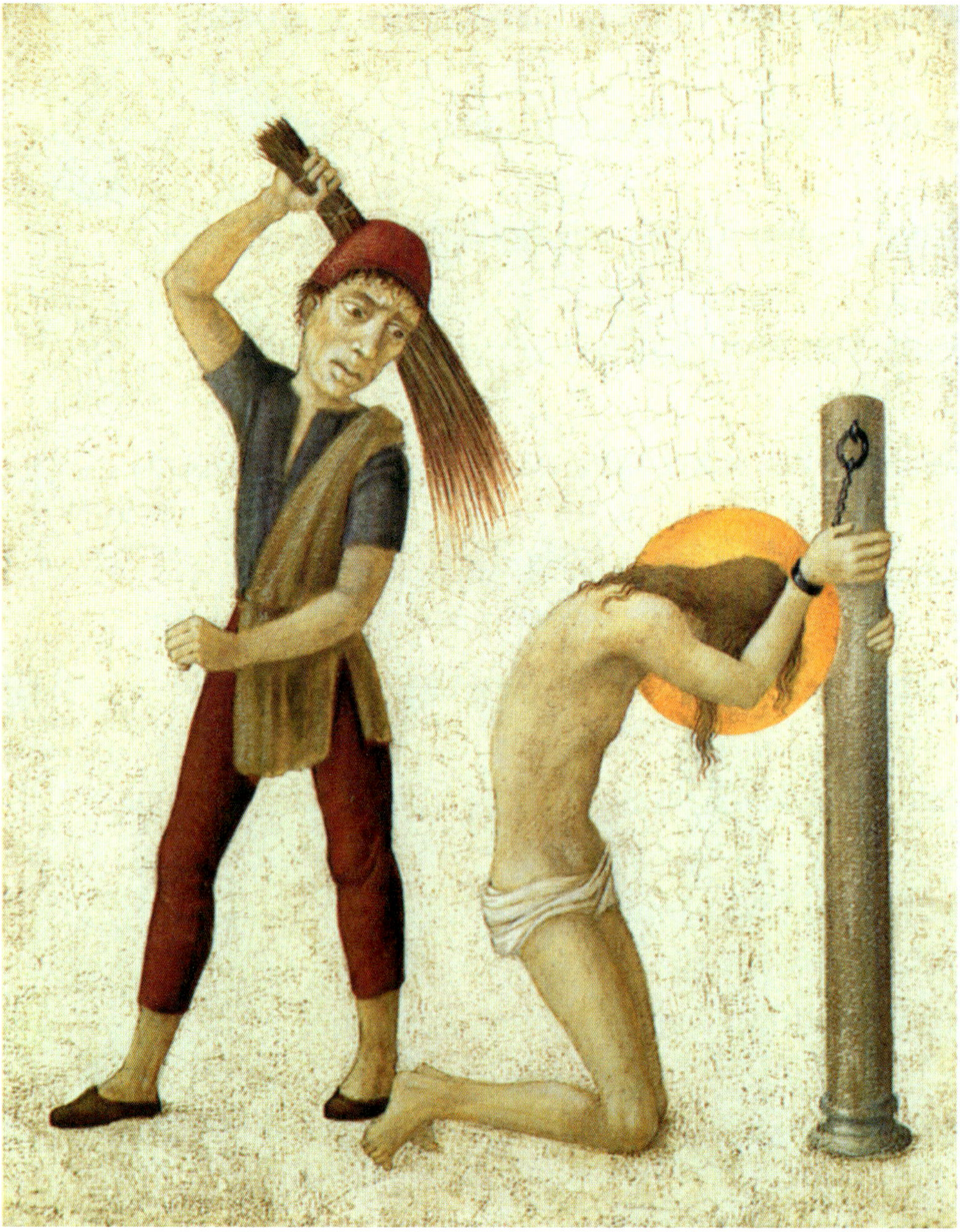

The Scourging at the Pillar

Virtue: Wanting What Jesus Wants

OUR FATHER

The next day, the soldiers brought Jesus to the leaders. *HAIL MARY...*

The leaders wanted to kill Jesus because He said He was the Son of God; they were jealous of Him. *HAIL MARY...*

The soldiers chained Jesus to a pillar and whipped Him many times. *HAIL MARY...*

Jesus accepted this suffering to free us from our sins. *HAIL MARY...*

Jesus loved and helped us by making a gift of Himself even though it hurt. *HAIL MARY...*

Jesus wants us to love and help others even when it doesn't feel good. *HAIL MARY...*

Sometimes we behave selfishly by caring more about what we want than helping those around us. *HAIL MARY...*

The Holy Spirit gives us the grace to overcome our selfish desires and to do the right thing. *HAIL MARY...*

Lord Jesus, thank you for your example of self-giving love. *HAIL MARY...*

God, our loving Father, please help us to want only what Jesus wants. *HAIL MARY...*

GLORY BE...FATIMA PRAYER (OH MY JESUS)...

The Sorrowful Mysteries

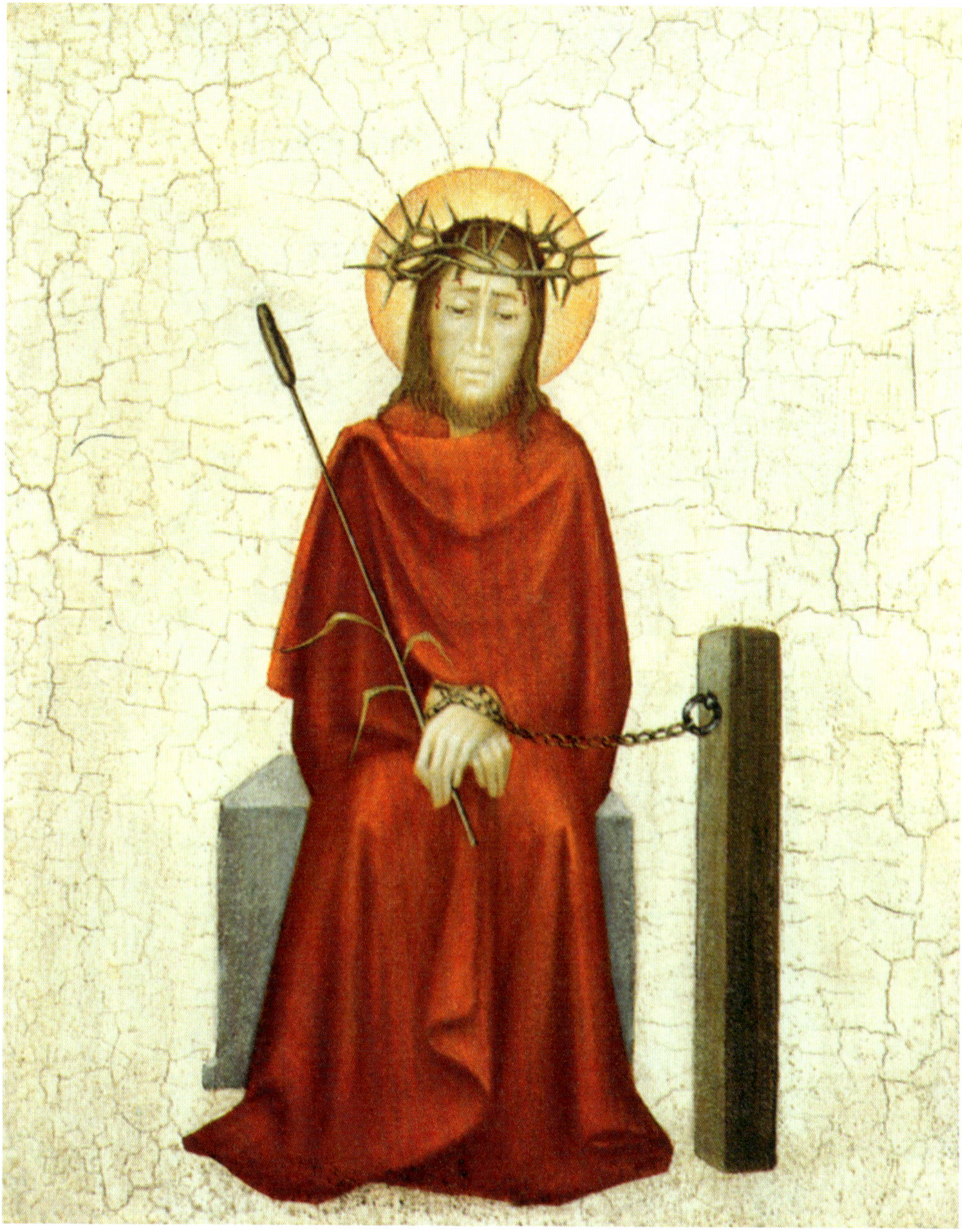

The Crowning with Thorns

Virtue: Endurance

OUR FATHER

The soldiers made fun of Jesus by dressing Him in a purple robe and pressing a painful crown of thorns on His head. *HAIL MARY...*

The soldiers spat on Jesus and mocked Him. *HAIL MARY...*

The soldiers wanted to punish and hurt Jesus, even though He had never done anything hurtful to anyone. *HAIL MARY...*

Jesus did not fight back, even though He was God and could have stopped them from hurting Him. *HAIL MARY...*

Jesus suffered this cruel treatment to free us from our sins. *HAIL MARY...*

Jesus accepted this cruel treatment because He loves us. *HAIL MARY...*

Jesus wants us to do the right thing even when others might treat us badly for doing so. *HAIL MARY...*

To help us choose what is good and right, God offers us special help through the power and grace of the Holy Spirit. *HAIL MARY...*

Lord Jesus, thank you for your example of always doing good to others. *HAIL MARY...*

God, our loving Father, please give us the endurance we need to do the right thing. *HAIL MARY...*

GLORY BE...FATIMA PRAYER (OH MY JESUS)...

The Sorrowful Mysteries

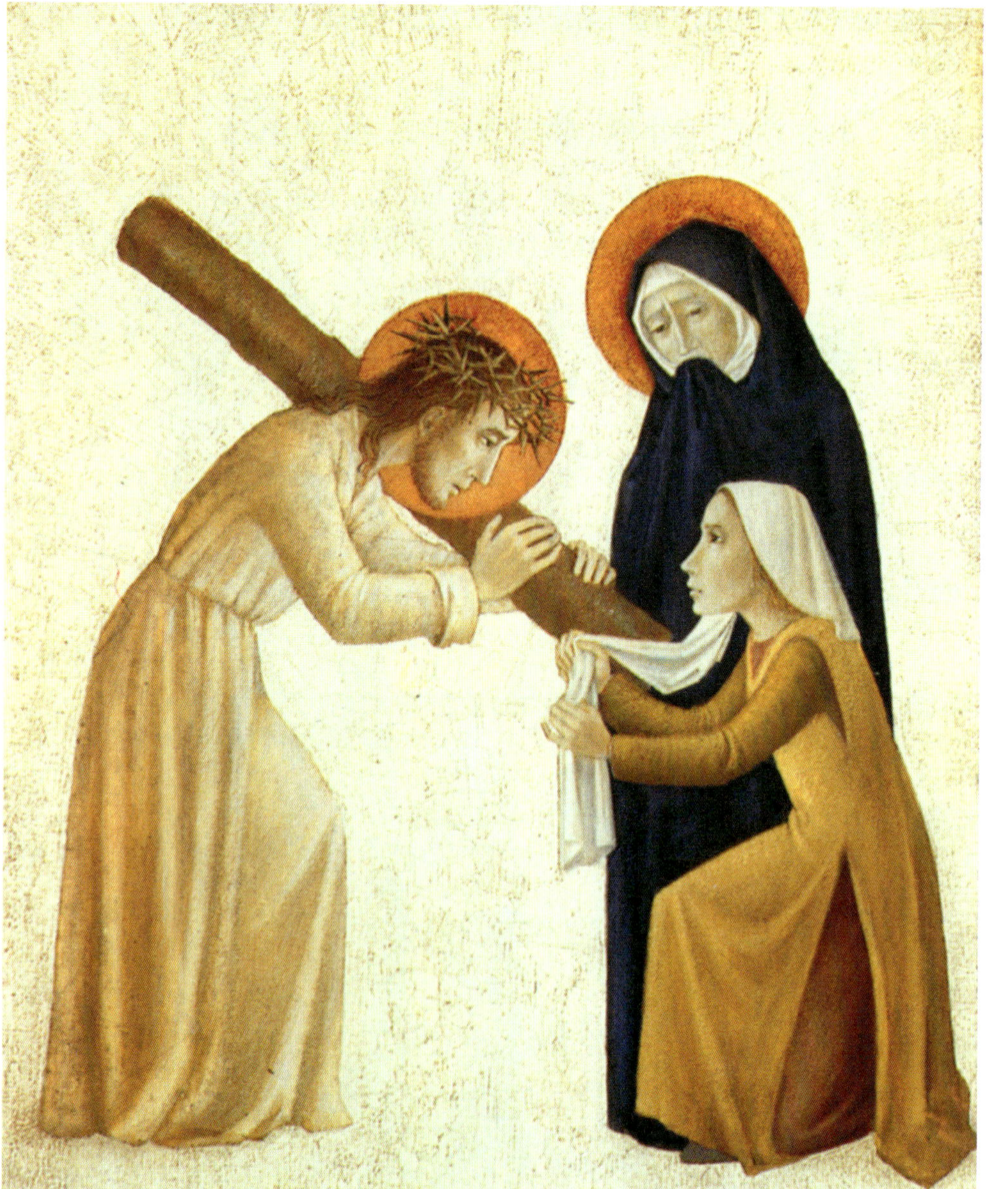

The Carrying of the Cross

Virtue: Carrying Our Cross With the Help of Jesus

OUR FATHER

After crowning Him with thorns, the soldiers made Jesus carry a heavy cross through the streets and up a hill. *HAIL MARY...*

Jesus was so weary from being mistreated that He fell three times. *HAIL MARY...*

The soldiers forced a man named Simon to help Jesus. *HAIL MARY...*

Simon made a gift of himself by helping Jesus carry His cross. *HAIL MARY...*

Our crosses are the things that burden us, cause us pain, and make us feel sad. *HAIL MARY...*

Jesus loves us and wants to help us carry our crosses. *HAIL MARY...*

Our crosses become lighter and easier to bear when we invite Jesus to help us. *HAIL MARY...*

Jesus wants us to unite our suffering with His so we can help others. *HAIL MARY...*

Lord Jesus, thank you for helping us to carry our crosses. *HAIL MARY...*

God, our loving Father, please help us to use our suffering as an opportunity to love and to be a gift to others. *HAIL MARY...*

GLORY BE...FATIMA PRAYER (OH MY JESUS)...

The Sorrowful Mysteries

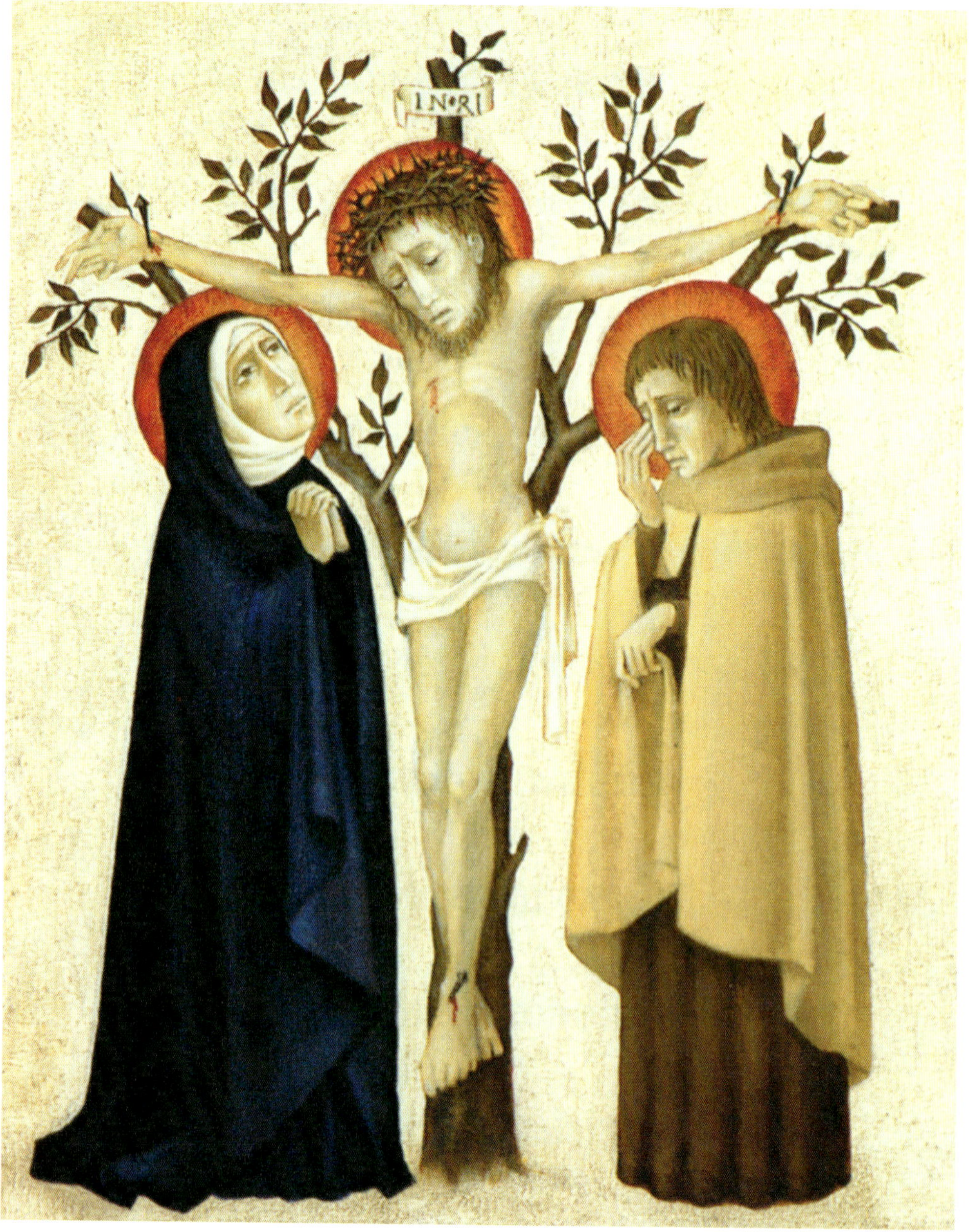
I N RI

The Crucifixion

Virtue: Self-Gift

OUR FATHER

The soldiers led Jesus to the top of the hill and nailed Him to the cross. *HAIL MARY...*

Jesus suffered terribly on the cross before He died. *HAIL MARY...*

Jesus accepted His suffering in order to free us from our sins. *HAIL MARY...*

Jesus gave His life so we could go to Heaven. *HAIL MARY...*

Jesus made a gift of Himself on the cross. *HAIL MARY...*

Jesus' gift on the cross is the greatest gift anyone has ever given. *HAIL MARY...*

Jesus put His Father and us before Himself. *HAIL MARY...*

When we love, we want what is good for the other person, and we put God and others first. *HAIL MARY...*

Lord Jesus, thank you for showing us how to love even when you were in so much pain. *HAIL MARY...*

God, our loving Father, please help us to follow your two greatest commandments: to love you and to love one another. *HAIL MARY...*

GLORY BE...FATIMA PRAYER (OH MY JESUS)...

The Sorrowful Mysteries

The Glorious Mysteries

Wednesday & Sunday

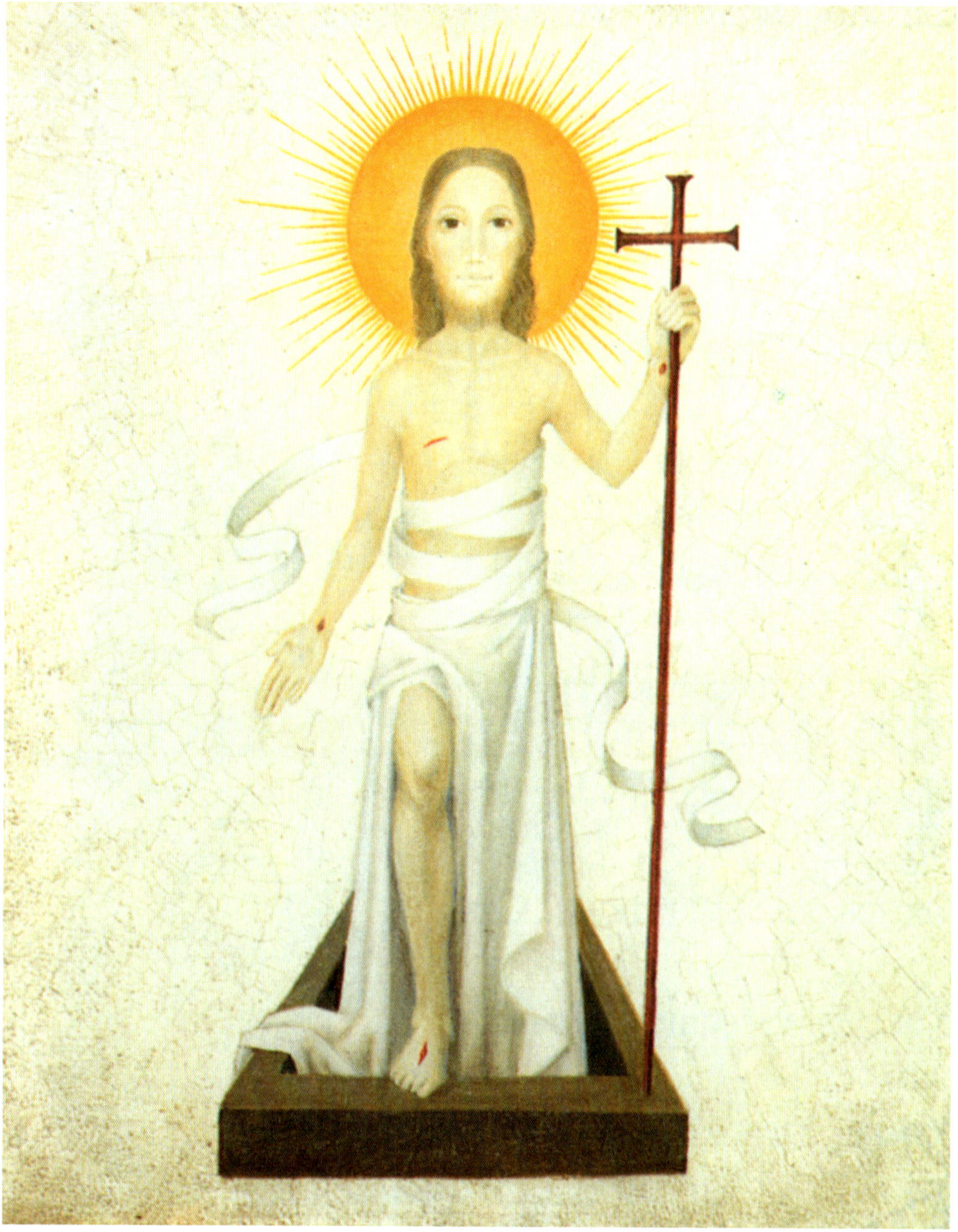

The Resurrection

Virtue: Faith

OUR FATHER

Three days after Jesus died, He rose from the dead and His body and soul were reunited. *HAIL MARY...*

Jesus' Resurrection is the most important event in the history of the world. *HAIL MARY...*

Jesus appeared to many people after His Resurrection. *HAIL MARY...*

Jesus' friends could see, touch, and hear Him, but there was something different about His body. *HAIL MARY...*

Jesus' body was glorified, just like at the Transfiguration. *HAIL MARY...*

Even though Jesus had told His friends that He would be resurrected, some of them did not have faith that it would happen. *HAIL MARY...*

Sometimes it is hard to have faith and believe in things we cannot see. *HAIL MARY...*

God gives us the gift of faith, and the Holy Spirit helps us to trust in this gift. *HAIL MARY...*

God, our loving Father, thank you for the Resurrection of Jesus. *HAIL MARY...*

God, our loving Father, please help us to grow in our faith and to share it with others. *HAIL MARY...*

GLORY BE...FATIMA PRAYER (OH MY JESUS)...

The Glorious Mysteries

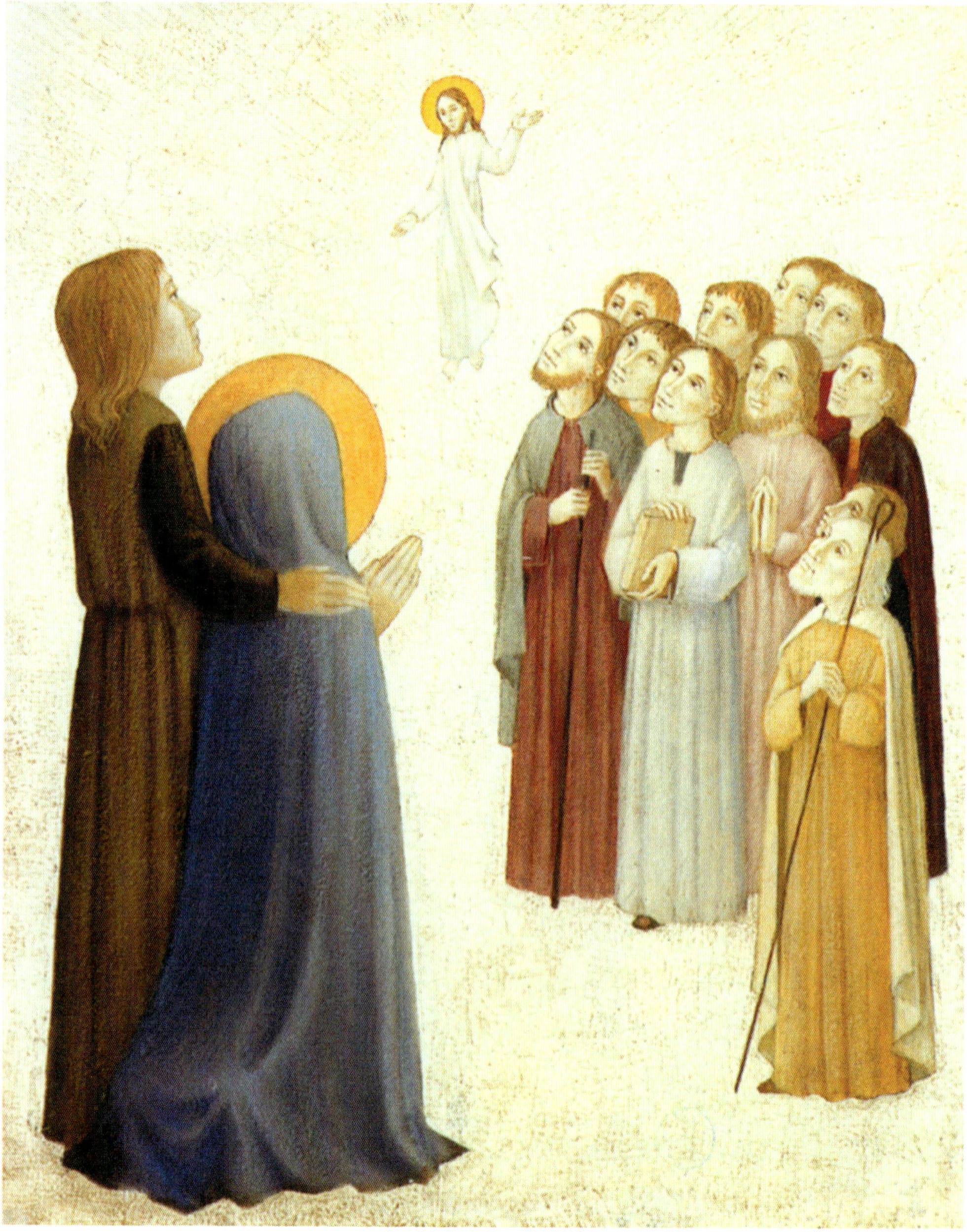

The Ascension

Virtue: Desire for Heaven

OUR FATHER

Forty days after His Resurrection, Jesus ascended into Heaven, body and soul. *HAIL MARY...*

Jesus said that He was going to prepare a place in Heaven for those who follow Him. *HAIL MARY...*

Jesus wants to lead us to Heaven. *HAIL MARY...*

God made us so He could share His love with each one of us in Heaven forever. *HAIL MARY...*

In Heaven, our body and our soul will be reunited. *HAIL MARY...*

In Heaven, we will be happier than we could ever imagine. *HAIL MARY...*

In Heaven, we will see God face to face. *HAIL MARY...*

In Heaven, we will love perfectly. *HAIL MARY...*

Lord Jesus, thank you for preparing a place in Heaven for us. *HAIL MARY...*

God, our loving Father, please help us to grow in our desire to see you in Heaven. *HAIL MARY...*

GLORY BE...FATIMA PRAYER (OH MY JESUS)...

The Glorious Mysteries

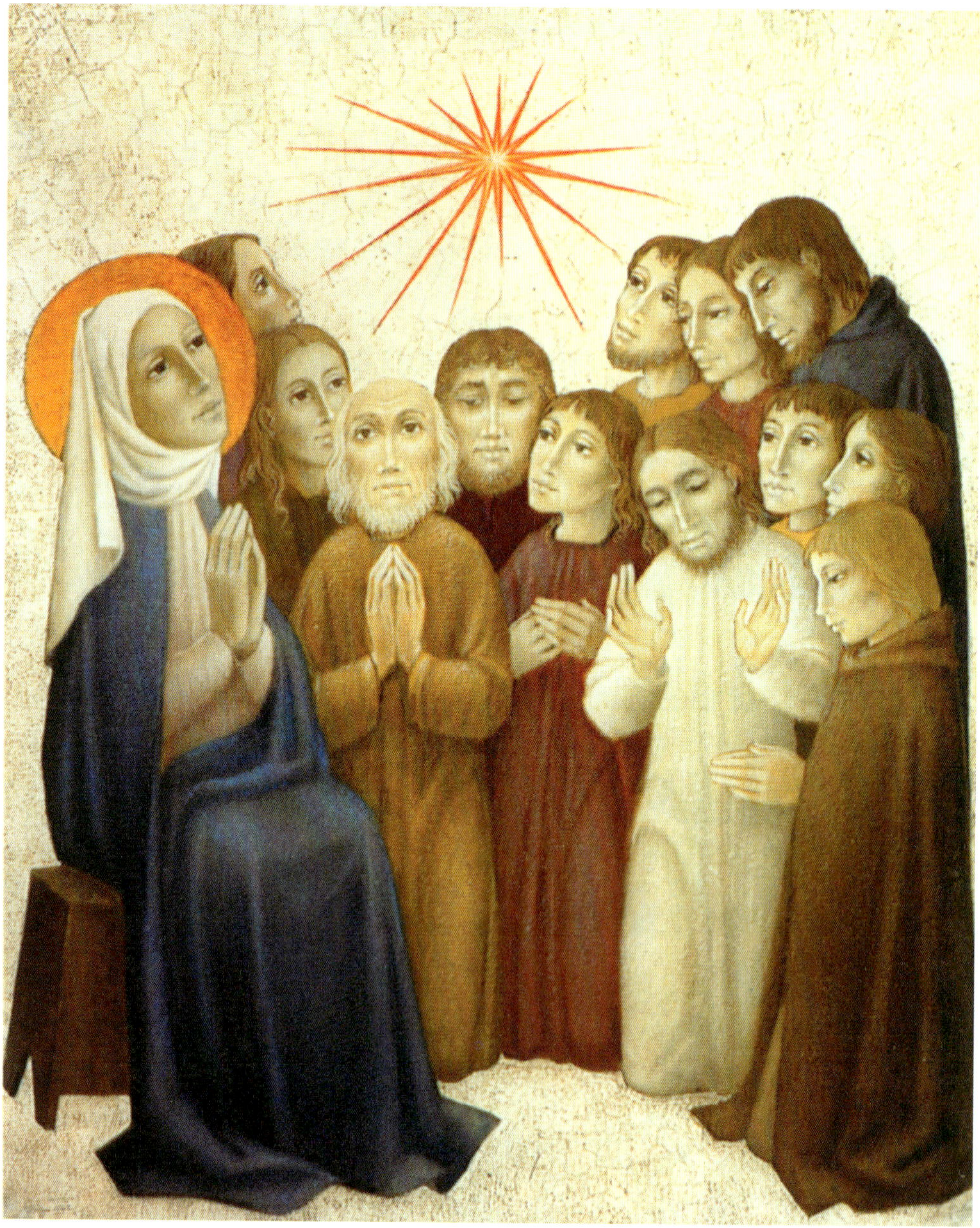

The Descent of the Holy Spirit

Virtue: Openness to the Holy Spirit

OUR FATHER

After ascending into Heaven, Jesus sent the Holy Spirit upon Mary and His apostles. *HAIL MARY...*

The Holy Spirit came to Mary and the apostles with the sound of a great wind and with tongues of fire, which rested upon each one of them. *HAIL MARY...*

On that day when the Holy Spirit came, the Catholic Church was born. *HAIL MARY...*

The Holy Spirit gave the apostles strength to make Jesus known throughout the world. *HAIL MARY...*

As members of the Catholic Church, we have been given the same task. *HAIL MARY...*

When we were baptized, we received the Holy Spirit for the first time. *HAIL MARY...*

When we are confirmed, we receive the Holy Spirit again with even more gifts from God. *HAIL MARY...*

The Holy Spirit gives us the power to make good choices so that we can be truly happy. *HAIL MARY...*

God, our loving Father, thank you for the gift of the Holy Spirit in our lives. *HAIL MARY...*

God, our loving Father, please help us to accept the help of the Holy Spirit and share His gifts with others. *HAIL MARY...*

GLORY BE...FATIMA PRAYER (OH MY JESUS)...

The Glorious Mysteries

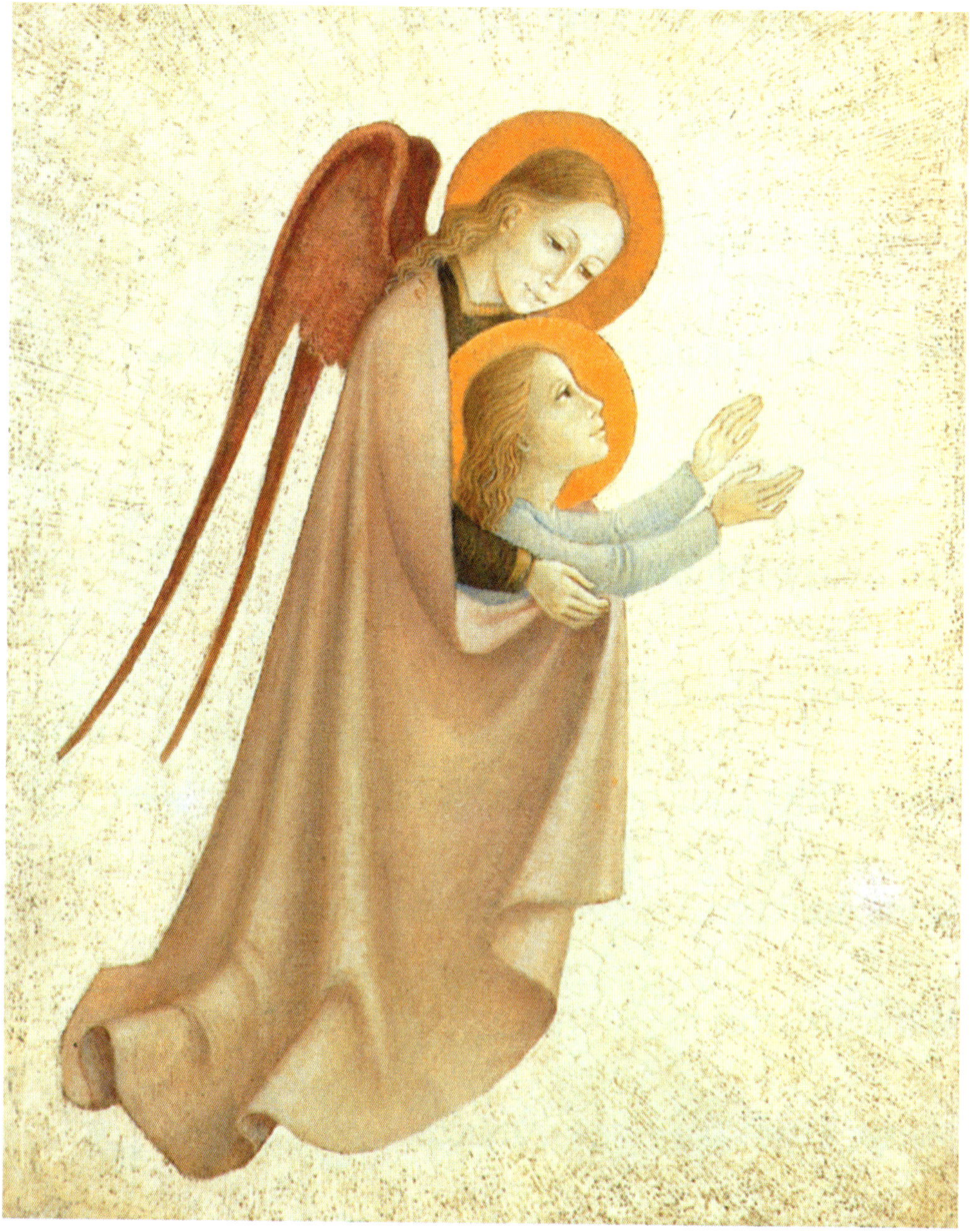

The Assumption

Virtue: Love for Mary

OUR FATHER

At the end of her life, Jesus wanted to give Mary a special gift. *HAIL MARY...*

Mary was assumed to heavenly glory, body and soul, by the power of God. *HAIL MARY...*

Jesus and Mary were happy to be together again forever. *HAIL MARY...*

Mary's glorious Assumption shows us the dignity of our bodies. *HAIL MARY...*

Mary helps us to respect our bodies and the bodies of others. *HAIL MARY...*

Mary always watches over us and protects us with the tender loving care of a mother. *HAIL MARY...*

Mary is Jesus' mother and our mother too. *HAIL MARY...*

Mary helps us to know and love Jesus. *HAIL MARY...*

Lord Jesus, thank you for giving us your mother so she can be our mother too. *HAIL MARY...*

God, our loving Father, please help us to know and love Mary more and more each day. *HAIL MARY...*

GLORY BE...FATIMA PRAYER (OH MY JESUS)...

The Glorious Mysteries

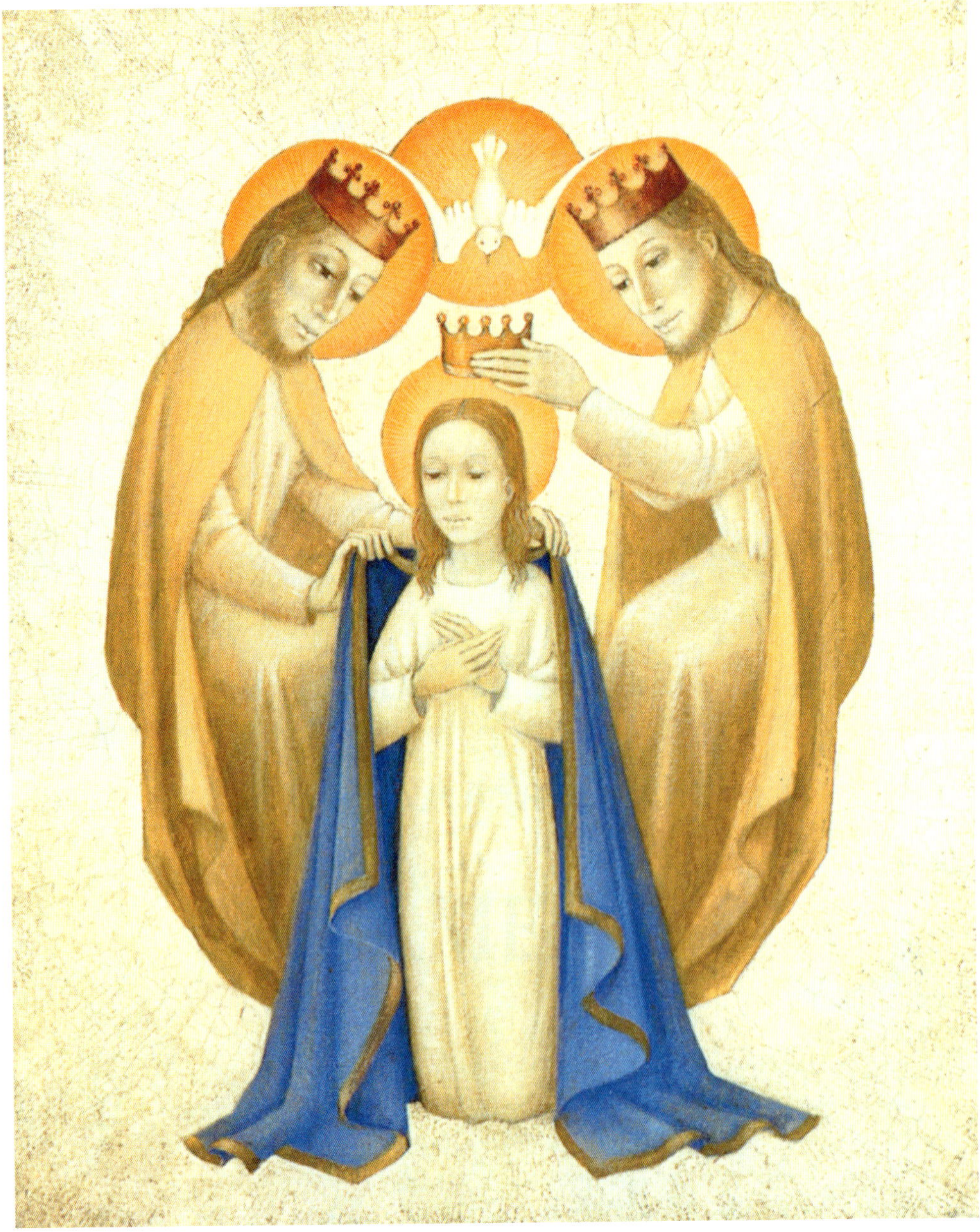

The Coronation

Virtue: Trust in Mary

OUR FATHER

After her Assumption into Heaven, Mary was crowned as Queen of Heaven and Earth. *HAIL MARY...*

Mary was rewarded for her perfect example of love and for sharing in Jesus' sufferings. *HAIL MARY...*

God wants us to be like Jesus and Mary so we can join them one day in Heaven. *HAIL MARY...*

We can learn from the saints to be close to Mary and act as she did. *HAIL MARY...*

Mary loves Jesus and each one of us perfectly. *HAIL MARY...*

Mary prays for us and watches over us as our mother. *HAIL MARY...*

Mary asks Jesus to give us graces when we need them. *HAIL MARY...*

Jesus wants us to ask Mary for His graces. *HAIL MARY...*

Lord Jesus, thank you for giving us your mother as Queen of Heaven and Earth. *HAIL MARY...*

God, our loving Father, please help us to trust that Mary will lead us to Jesus and help us get to Heaven. *HAIL MARY...*

GLORY BE...FATIMA PRAYER (OH MY JESUS)...

The Glorious Mysteries

The Luminous Mysteries

Thursday

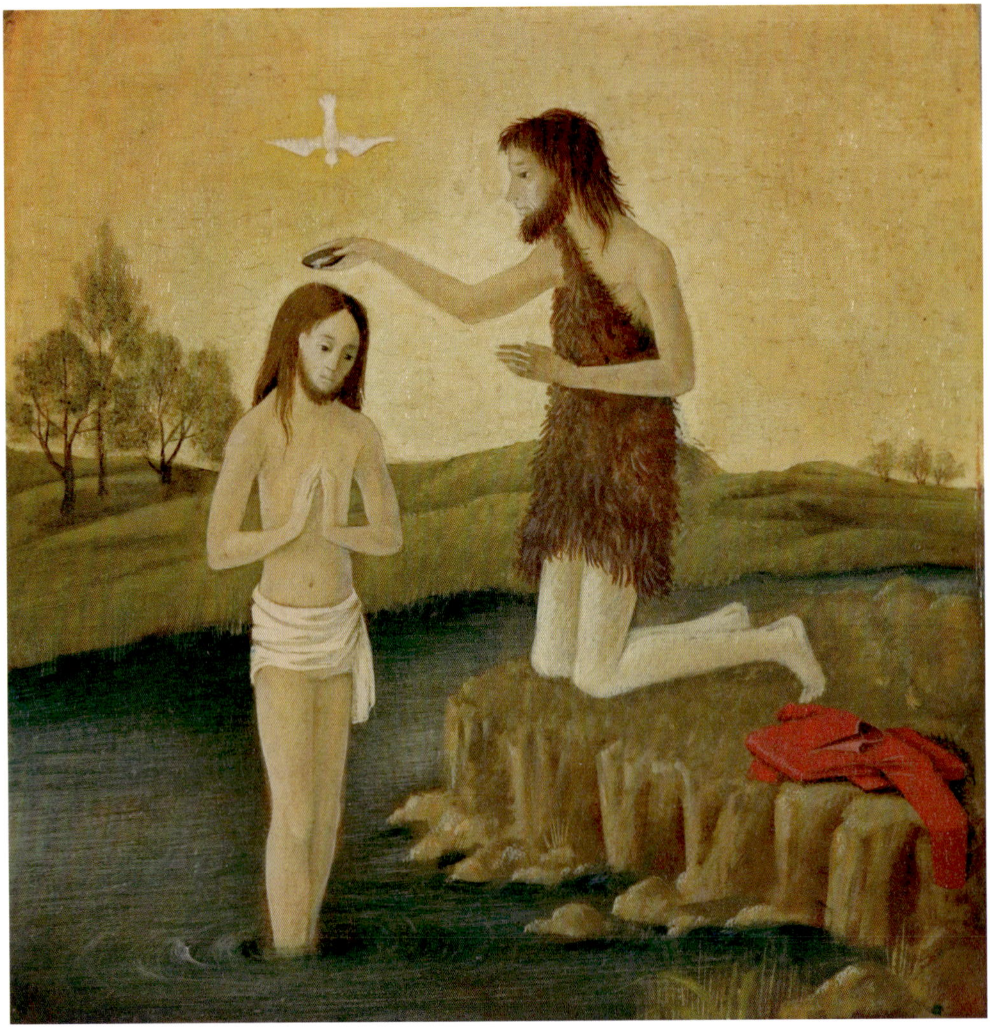

The Baptism of Jesus

Virtue: Preparing Our Heart for Jesus

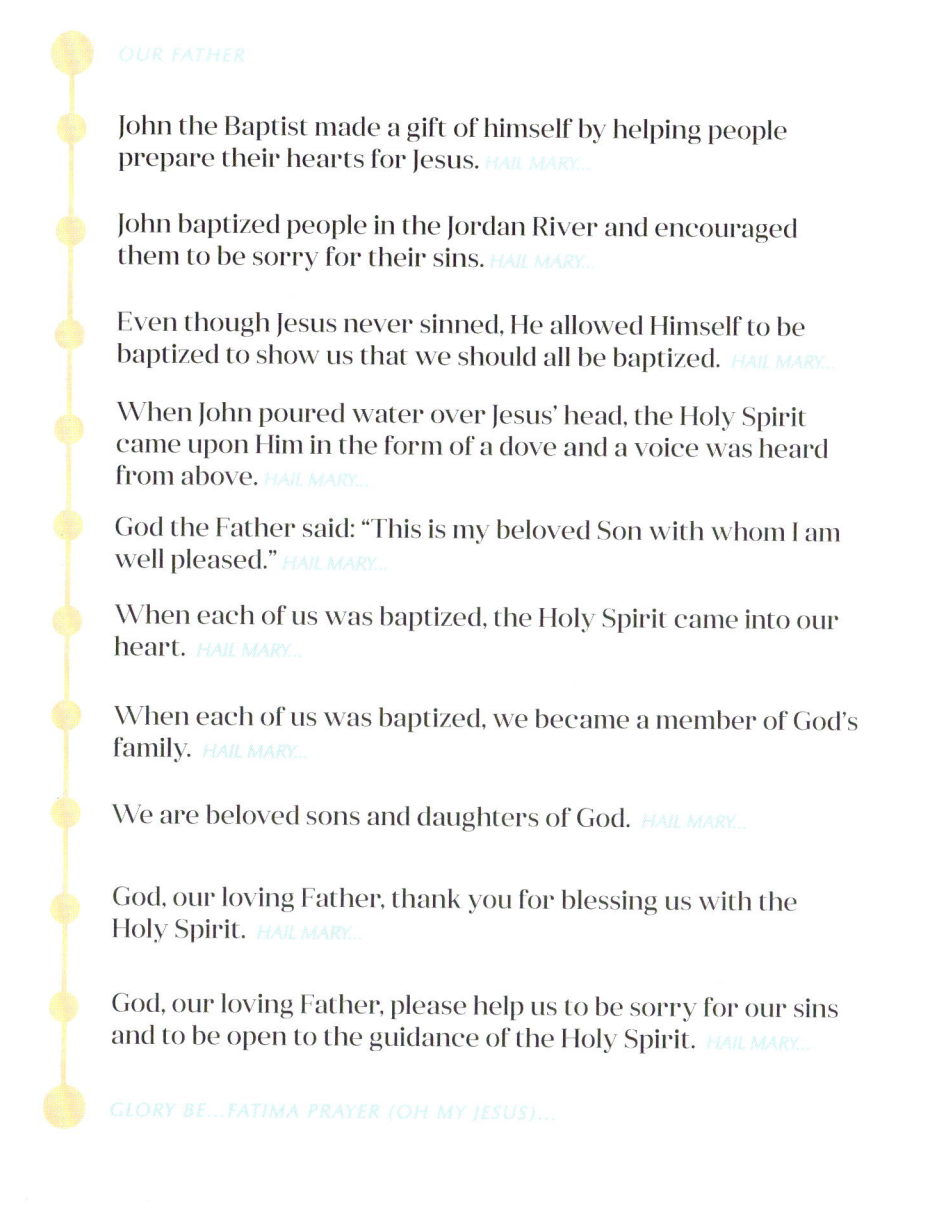

OUR FATHER

John the Baptist made a gift of himself by helping people prepare their hearts for Jesus. *HAIL MARY...*

John baptized people in the Jordan River and encouraged them to be sorry for their sins. *HAIL MARY...*

Even though Jesus never sinned, He allowed Himself to be baptized to show us that we should all be baptized. *HAIL MARY...*

When John poured water over Jesus' head, the Holy Spirit came upon Him in the form of a dove and a voice was heard from above. *HAIL MARY...*

God the Father said: "This is my beloved Son with whom I am well pleased." *HAIL MARY...*

When each of us was baptized, the Holy Spirit came into our heart. *HAIL MARY...*

When each of us was baptized, we became a member of God's family. *HAIL MARY...*

We are beloved sons and daughters of God. *HAIL MARY...*

God, our loving Father, thank you for blessing us with the Holy Spirit. *HAIL MARY...*

God, our loving Father, please help us to be sorry for our sins and to be open to the guidance of the Holy Spirit. *HAIL MARY...*

GLORY BE...FATIMA PRAYER (OH MY JESUS)...

The Luminous Mysteries

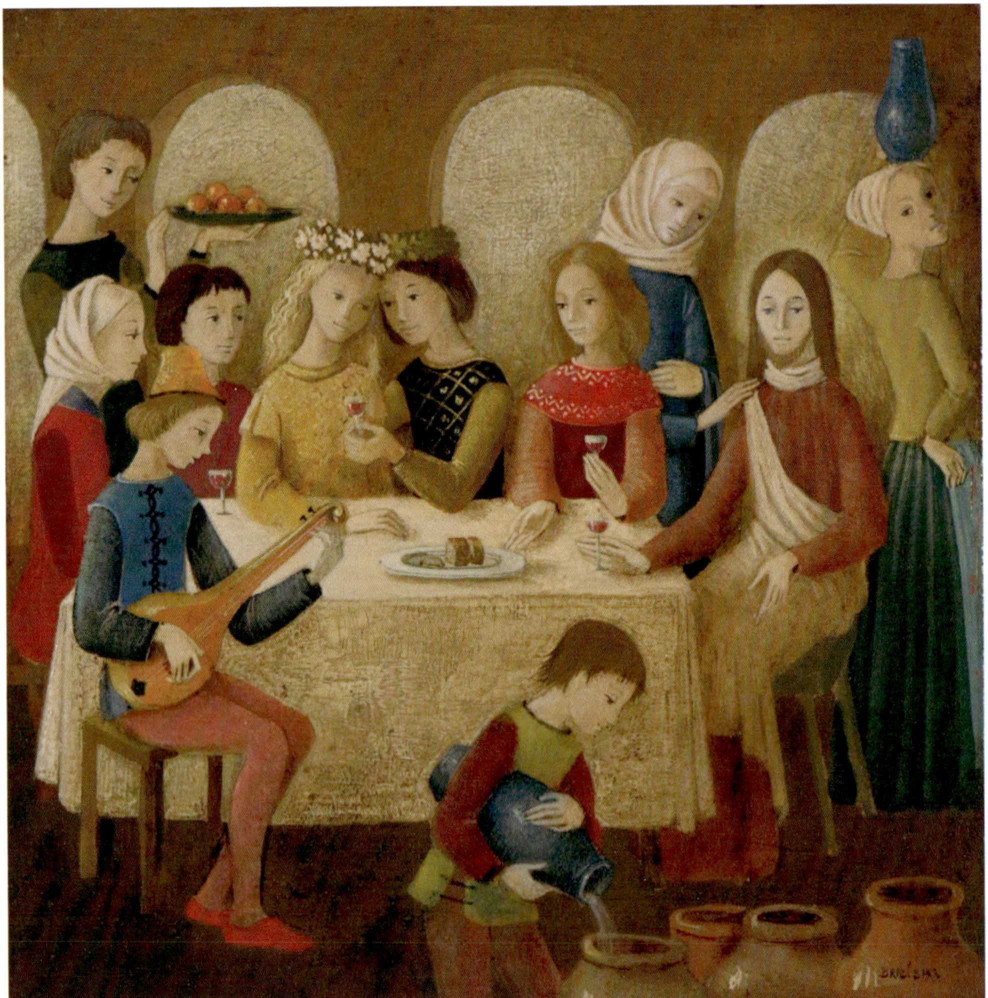

The Wedding Feast at Cana

Virtue: Loving God's Plan for Our Lives

OUR FATHER

One day, Jesus and Mary went to a wedding feast in a town called Cana. *HAIL MARY...*

Mary made sure to let Jesus know that the bride and groom had no more wine for their wedding feast. *HAIL MARY...*

The people were amazed when Jesus turned water into wine. *HAIL MARY...*

Turning the water into wine was Jesus' first miracle. *HAIL MARY...*

Jesus' miracle at the wedding is God's way of showing us that marriage is important. *HAIL MARY...*

When a man and woman get married, they promise to treat each other as gifts and help each other get to Heaven. *HAIL MARY...*

With His grace, God helps a husband and a wife to love each other. *HAIL MARY...*

God has a loving plan for each of us that He will reveal to us in our hearts. *HAIL MARY...*

God, our loving Father, thank you for the gift of marriage. *HAIL MARY...*

God, our loving Father, please help us to recognize your voice speaking in our hearts. *HAIL MARY...*

GLORY BE...FATIMA PRAYER (OH MY JESUS)...

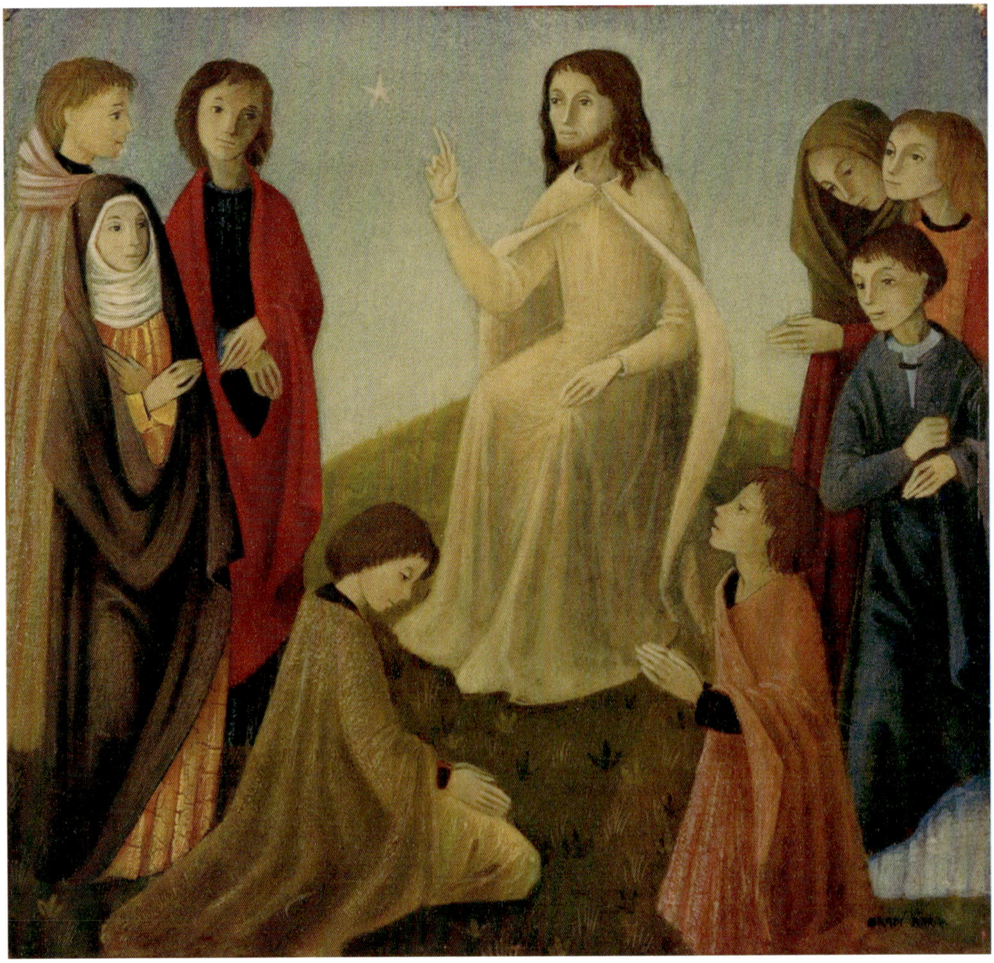

The Proclamation of the Kingdom

Virtue: Desire to be Like Jesus

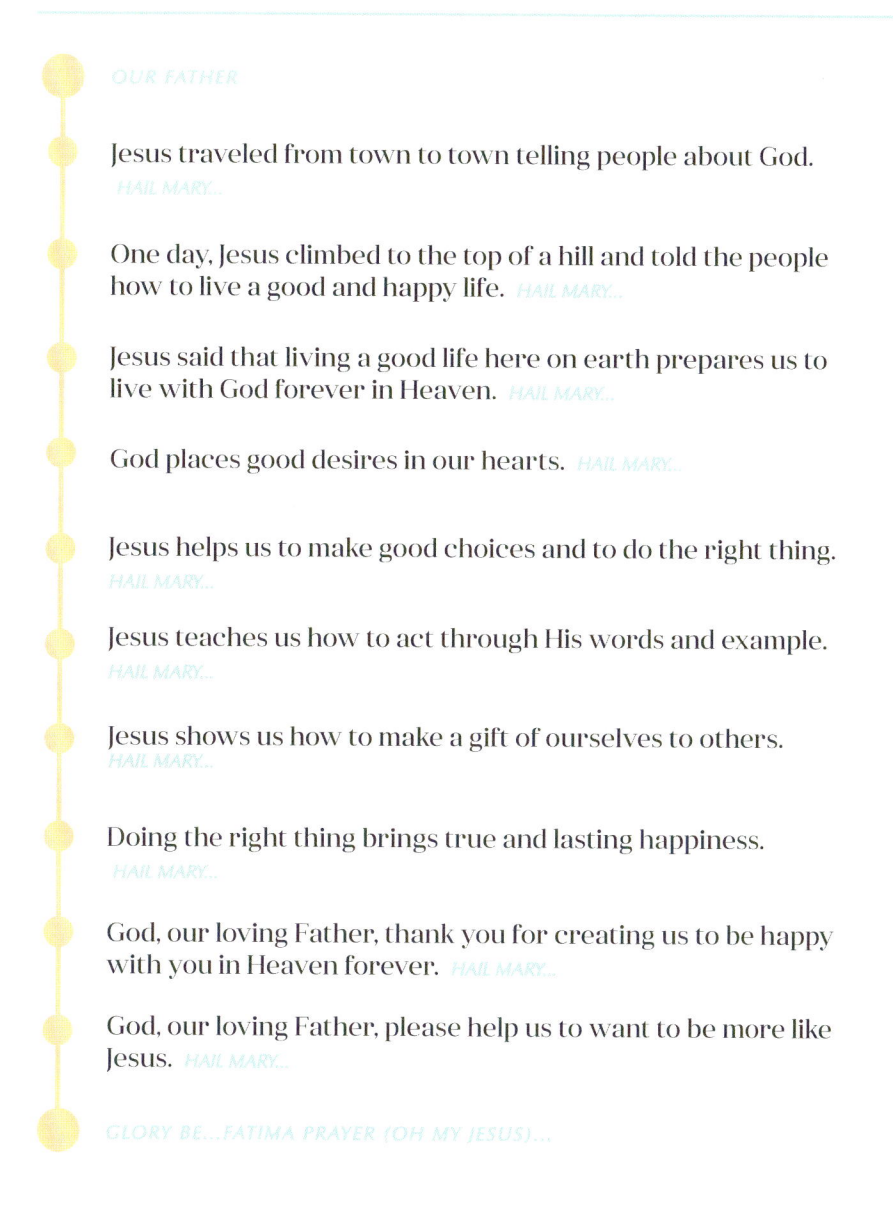

OUR FATHER...

Jesus traveled from town to town telling people about God. *HAIL MARY...*

One day, Jesus climbed to the top of a hill and told the people how to live a good and happy life. *HAIL MARY...*

Jesus said that living a good life here on earth prepares us to live with God forever in Heaven. *HAIL MARY...*

God places good desires in our hearts. *HAIL MARY...*

Jesus helps us to make good choices and to do the right thing. *HAIL MARY...*

Jesus teaches us how to act through His words and example. *HAIL MARY...*

Jesus shows us how to make a gift of ourselves to others. *HAIL MARY...*

Doing the right thing brings true and lasting happiness. *HAIL MARY...*

God, our loving Father, thank you for creating us to be happy with you in Heaven forever. *HAIL MARY...*

God, our loving Father, please help us to want to be more like Jesus. *HAIL MARY...*

GLORY BE...FATIMA PRAYER (OH MY JESUS)...

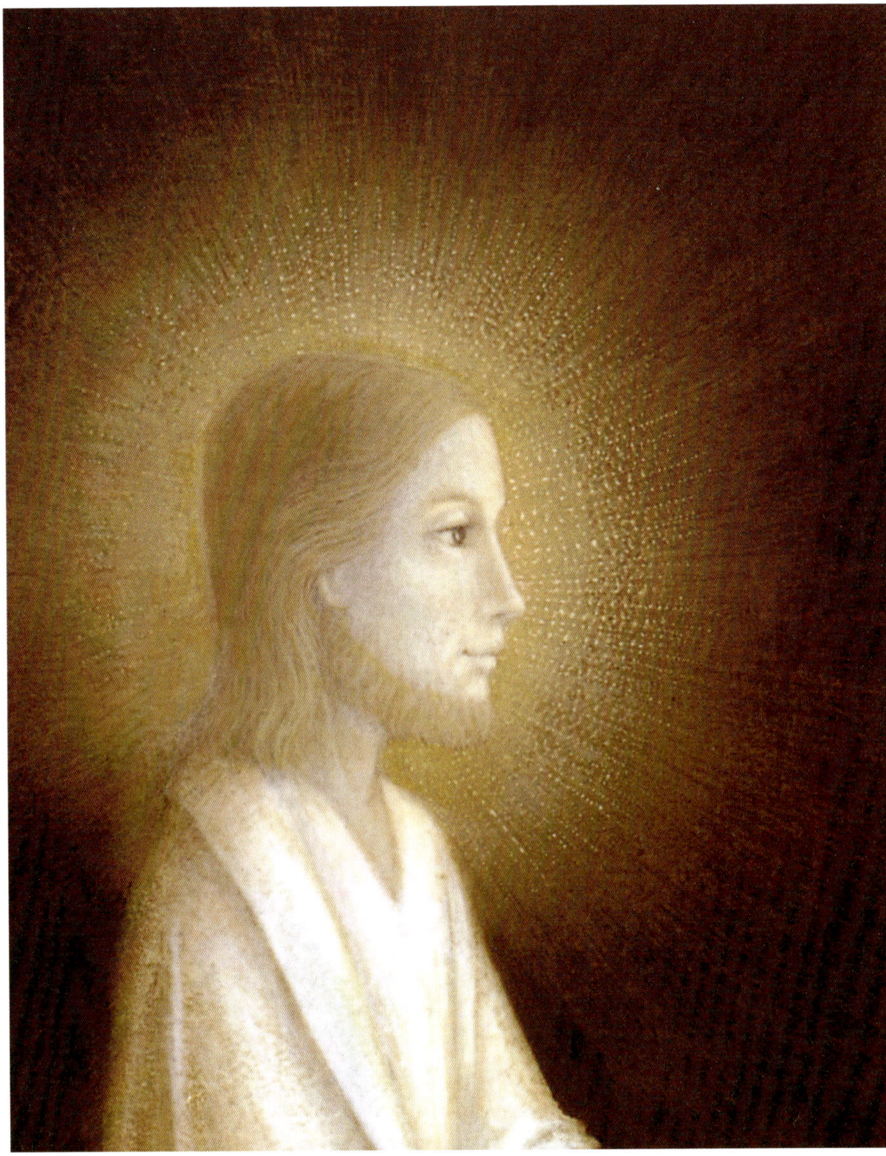

The Transfiguration

Virtue: Desire for a Gloried Body and Soul

OUR FATHER...

One day, Jesus took Peter, James, and John up on a mountain to pray. *HAIL MARY...*

On the mountain, Jesus was suddenly transfigured. *HAIL MARY...*

Jesus' face glowed like the sun and His clothes became dazzling white. *HAIL MARY...*

The apostles were frightened to see this change, but Jesus comforted them and told them not to be afraid. *HAIL MARY...*

Jesus was showing the apostles how His body would look in Heaven. *HAIL MARY...*

Jesus was preparing the apostles for Heaven by showing them what their bodies would be like when they got there. *HAIL MARY...*

God will give a glorified body and soul to everyone who follows Jesus to Heaven. *HAIL MARY...*

By acting like Jesus and obeying Him, we make ourselves more ready for Heaven. *HAIL MARY...*

Lord Jesus, thank you for showing us how beautiful Heaven will be. *HAIL MARY...*

God, our loving Father, please help us to see your glory and to be filled with hope for Heaven. *HAIL MARY...*

GLORY BE...FATIMA PRAYER (OH MY JESUS)...

The Luminous Mysteries

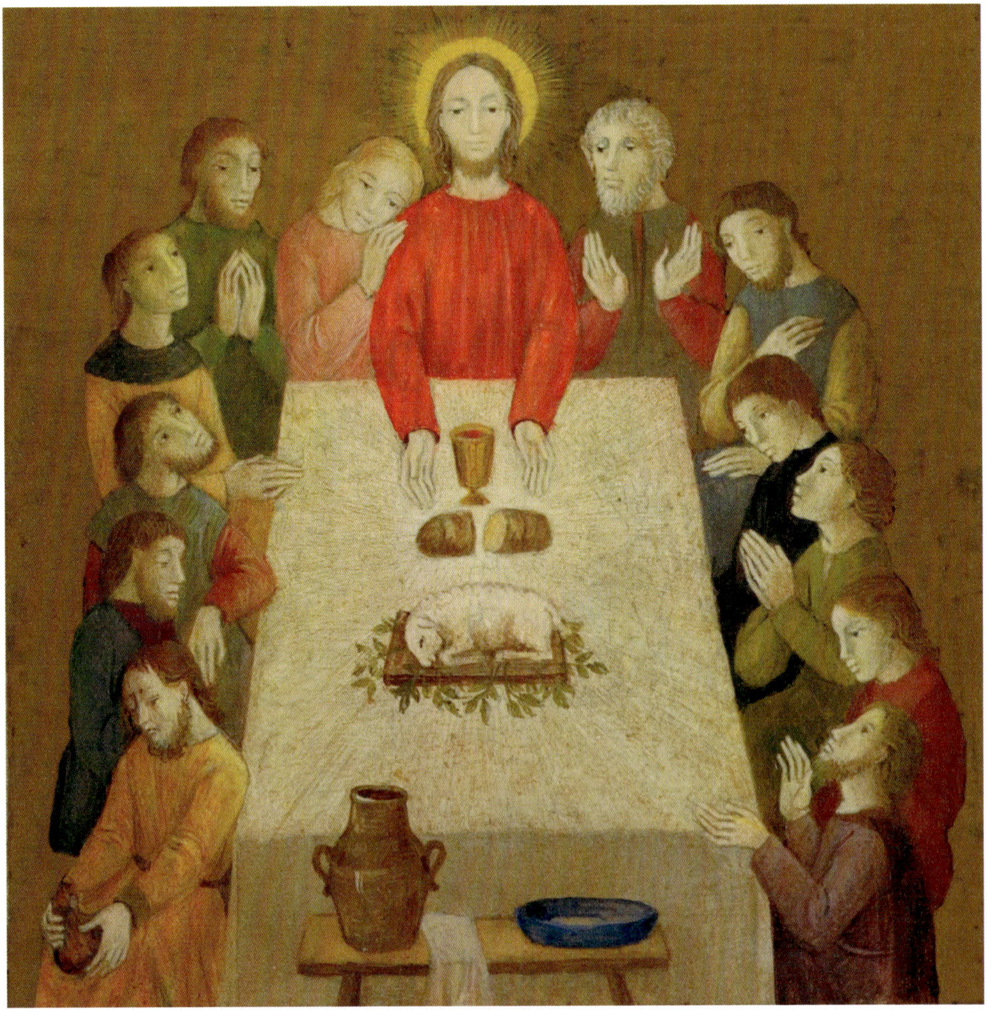

The Institution of the Eucharist

Virtue: Love for Jesus in the Eucharist

OUR FATHER

On the night before Jesus was crucified, He shared one last meal with His apostles. *HAIL MARY...*

While they were eating, Jesus took bread, blessed it, and gave it to them, saying, "This is my body." *HAIL MARY...*

Then, Jesus took wine and said, "This is my blood." *HAIL MARY...*

During the Last Supper, Jesus gave Himself to us in the Eucharist for the first time. *HAIL MARY...*

The Eucharist is the greatest gift on earth. *HAIL MARY...*

Jesus offers the gift of Himself to us in the Eucharist every time we celebrate Mass. *HAIL MARY...*

Jesus wants us to receive the Eucharist with a joyful and grateful heart. *HAIL MARY...*

When we receive Jesus in the Eucharist, He gives us the grace to be more like Him and love God and others more. *HAIL MARY...*

Lord Jesus, thank you for giving us yourself through the gifts of the Mass and the Eucharist. *HAIL MARY...*

God, our loving Father, please help us to love Jesus in the Eucharist and welcome Him into our hearts when we receive Him. *HAIL MARY...*

GLORY BE...FATIMA PRAYER (OH MY JESUS)...

The Luminous Mysteries

ABOUT THE AUTHOR

Debbie Staresinic is a wife, mother, and grandmother, with a special love for the Blessed Mother and a passion for sharing the Church's beautiful vision concerning the meaning and value of the human person. Following the words and example of St. John Paul II, Mrs. Staresinic invites us to enter more fully into the Church's call to be active witnesses of Jesus Christ's sacrificial love in our lives. Mrs. Staresinic is also the author of:

Theology of the Body Rosary Meditations